CW01220129

Taking Offence on Social Media

Caroline Tagg · Philip Seargeant
Amy Aisha Brown

Taking Offence on Social Media

Conviviality and Communication on Facebook

palgrave
macmillan

Caroline Tagg
Languages and Applied Linguistics
Open University
Milton Keynes, UK

Amy Aisha Brown
The University of Nottingham Ningbo
Ningbo, China

Philip Seargeant
Languages and Applied Linguistics
Open University
Milton Keynes, UK

ISBN 978-3-319-56716-7   ISBN 978-3-319-56717-4 (eBook)
DOI 10.1007/978-3-319-56717-4

Library of Congress Control Number: 2017937280

© The Editor(s) (if applicable) and The Author(s) 2017
This work is subject to copyright. All rights are solely and exclusively licensed by the Publisher, whether the whole or part of the material is concerned, specifically the rights of translation, reprinting, reuse of illustrations, recitation, broadcasting, reproduction on microfilms or in any other physical way, and transmission or information storage and retrieval, electronic adaptation, computer software, or by similar or dissimilar methodology now known or hereafter developed.
The use of general descriptive names, registered names, trademarks, service marks, etc. in this publication does not imply, even in the absence of a specific statement, that such names are exempt from the relevant protective laws and regulations and therefore free for general use.
The publisher, the authors and the editors are safe to assume that the advice and information in this book are believed to be true and accurate at the date of publication. Neither the publisher nor the authors or the editors give a warranty, express or implied, with respect to the material contained herein or for any errors or omissions that may have been made. The publisher remains neutral with regard to jurisdictional claims in published maps and institutional affiliations.

Cover illustration: © nemesis2207/Fotolia.co.uk

Printed on acid-free paper

This Palgrave Macmillan imprint is published by Springer Nature
The registered company is Springer International Publishing AG
The registered company address is: Gewerbestrasse 11, 6330 Cham, Switzerland

Acknowledgements

We would like to thank Korina Giaxoglou and Theresa Lillis for their helpful and engaged feedback on our draft, as well as the anonymous external reviewer. Our thanks also go to the participants in our study for taking the time to speak with us and to answer our questions.

Contents

1 *Creating Facebook*: A Study of Online Conflict and Conviviality — 1

2 Online Communication as Context Design — 19

3 Giving and Taking Offence: Theoretical and Empirical Approaches — 43

4 Social Media and Intradiverse Networks — 53

5 The Impact of Intradiversity on Online Offence — 67

6 Constructing Conviviality in Online Interaction — 89

7 Afterword: Beyond Facebook — 113

Bibliography — 123

Index — 137

List of Figures

Fig. 4.1	Make-up of the researcher's Facebook network based on the different stages of her life trajectory	58
Fig. 4.2	Country of residence of respondents	59
Fig. 4.3	Languages other than English that respondents reported using on Facebook	60
Fig. 4.4	Age of respondents	61
Fig. 4.5	Number of Facebook Friends respondents have	62
Fig. 4.6	Number of Friends respondents regularly interact with on Facebook	62
Fig. 4.7	How often respondents go onto Facebook	63
Fig. 4.8	How often respondents post on Facebook	64
Fig. 4.9	Respondents' primary uses of Facebook	64

CHAPTER 1

Creating Facebook: A Study of Online Conflict and Conviviality

Abstract In introducing the new concept of *context design*, this book draws on data collected as part of a research project titled *Creating Facebook*. This introductory chapter outlines the aims and rationale of the book, explaining the issues it addresses and how it draws upon an empirical survey and interviews into the giving and taking of offence in order to explore and illustrate these issues. The chapter also provides the academic context for our investigation of online interaction, situating the book within the rapidly developing field of language and social media studies, and in relation to work on media ideologies and media ecology.

Keywords Affordances · Media ecology · Media ideologies Online survey · Social media

INTRODUCTION

This book introduces the concept of *context design* as a way of understanding online communication, and the extent to which users have the agency to shape the social media contexts in which they interact. In both evidencing and illustrating context design, the book draws on findings from a 2-year research project called *Creating Facebook: the management of conflict and the pursuit of online conviviality*, which elicited people's media and language ideologies through an empirical online survey and follow-up interviews involving Facebook users. The focus in this book is on occasions where our participants claimed to have been offended or to have offended others on Facebook, revealing the site to be shaped by both *intradiversity* and *online conviviality* (both of which we explain below). Acts of offence-taking and offence-giving on Facebook constitute an important gap in the research literature, despite a focus on online aggression in more public sites such as Twitter and YouTube, and despite the prominent role played by Facebook in contemporary social and political life. As we explain below, understanding how and why offence occurs not only feeds into current discussions about online debate and civic discourse, but also reveals how people actively (re-)design the online context as they respond to perceived instances of miscommunication. In other words, the project findings act as a heuristic for understanding context design.

In this introductory chapter, we set out the socio-political and academic contexts for our investigation of online interaction, situating the book within the rapidly developing field of language and social media studies, and in relation to work on media ideologies and media ecology. We also elaborate on the aims, rationale and methodology of *Creating Facebook*, explaining the issues it addresses and how we draw upon the empirical survey and interview data relating to the giving and taking of offence in order to explore and illustrate these issues.

THE SOCIAL SIGNIFICANCE OF TAKING OFFENCE ON FACEBOOK

(1) I avoid posting things that I know will offend some people because I don't like offending people. I don't feel Facebook is the best place to discuss different viewpoints due to its public nature and the very mixed audience who would be reading my posts. I would rather discuss different opinions in real life when someone random isn't likely to join in. [Q24–76]

The ways in which people behave on social media sites are of great social and political importance in today's society. This is frequently illustrated in stories in the news, such as to pick just a couple of examples, the sexist bullying experienced on Twitter by the journalist Caroline Criado-Perez who campaigned for Jane Austen to be the new face on the £10 banknote in the UK (e.g. Doward 2013); the discussion and debate around users' reactions to racist comments posted on Facebook during the so-called European migration crisis of 2016 (e.g. *Independent* 2016); and the apparent spread of fake news across Facebook during the 2016 US Presidential elections (Solon 2016). While the last in particular raised questions regarding the way social media sites are designed—with particular attention paid to the role played by Facebook's 'personalisation algorithm' (which pushes particular content onto a user's newsfeed)—also central to such debates are questions regarding appropriate norms of behaviour on various social media platforms (and how these should be promoted and regulated), as well as differing ideas about the acceptability of voicing what can be (either by intention or accident) views which other people find offensive. In the quote above, which is taken from one of the responses to the survey undertaken as part of our research project, *Creating Facebook*, the respondent talks specifically of trying to avoid offending others when interacting with them on Facebook. She talks of how she draws a distinction between online interaction and 'real life', how she predicts the possible 'audience' for her posts, and how she has specific beliefs about what this particular social platform is best suited to—beliefs which then form the basis for what she herself does when communicating via Facebook. As can be seen, there is, even in this one short quote, a reflective awareness of the media, the way it is used and the role it has in the wider context of everyday life, which shapes how she approaches the social network site and how she manages her communication on it.

This book examines the nature of this reflective awareness, as expressed by the range of Facebook users whose views we elicited as part of *Creating Facebook*, in order to explore the role of social media in the contemporary social and political landscape. By focusing on the particular online interactional dynamics that give rise to the giving and taking of offence on Facebook—an issue which can act as a touchstone for more general notions of communication—the book aims to illuminate the challenges and hazards that people encounter in social media interactions, how people manage their communication on Facebook in the context of constantly evolving technologies, practices and social environments, and, in particular, the ways in which people's awareness of the affordances of new communicative technologies influence the way they conduct themselves online.

To examine how people manage the potential giving and taking of offence, the book draws on survey and interview data collected as part of *Creating Facebook*. The survey data comprises the responses of over a hundred people about their experiences of and beliefs about personal communication via their Facebook accounts, while the interview data includes more in-depth exploration of the views expressed by selected participants. Analysis of the participants' accounts across these datasets explores the way that communication on Facebook apparently gives rise to frequent examples of offence-giving which, we argue, is a result of the type of *intradiverse* community that Facebook facilitates. Intradiversity, which we discuss in details in Chap. 4, emerges from the type of 'ego-centred' network (Androutsopoulos 2014, p. 63) facilitated by personal Facebook profiles, whereby participation is to some extent structured around one user's personal connections, meaning that the diversity of a Facebook community is the product of, and to an extent constrained by, individual experiences and mutual friendships. The research shows that the participants in our project were most likely to be offended by particular types of post, namely, political, religious, sexist or racist opinions with which they disagreed. In the main, they accepted that some disagreement was inevitable, thus illustrating an awareness of the participant structure of Facebook, and for the most part simply ignored the offending posts. Where they did respond to things they took exception to they generally did so non-aggressively by ensuring through various methods that they no longer had access to such posts. These actions suggest that these Facebook users tend to be less interested in argument or conflict (of the kind described on sites like Twitter and YouTube) or indeed in more reasoned debate around differing views: as the respondent says in the quote at the top of the chapter, Facebook is not seen as a good forum for this type of interaction. Instead, two different scenarios appear typical. On the one hand, there is an attempt to construct a newsfeed filled only or predominantly with opinions with which they agree, a phenomenon that Jones and Hafner (2012, p. 126) call the 'ghetto-ization' of the Internet; on the other hand, there is a pattern of seeming indifference in that people will tolerate opposing views without challenging or engaging with them. The overall result is that *online conviviality*—the desire for peaceful coexistence online through negotiating or ignoring difference and avoiding contentious debate—appears to be an overarching principle for this particular type of 'ego-centred' social media encounter. As noted above, this is not the case for all social media platforms, however an issue we will return to at the end of the book.

In exploring offence for the insights, it offers into people's ideas about appropriate behaviour on Facebook and how their ideas may shape the type of communication that Facebook typically gives rise to, the book uses the examination of discursive constructions of online offence as a heuristic for theorising the analytic concept of *context design*, which we put forward as a key theoretical model for understanding online communication. Building on the concept of audience design (Bell 1984) and contemporary models of the interactive construction of context both offline (Duranti and Goodwin 1992) and online (Lyons 2014), context design highlights the ways in which social media users imagine and respond to a particularly complex set of contextual variables as they design their posts and interactions. As such, context design offers a powerful critique and refinement of the widely used yet relatively under-theorised concept of 'context collapse' which has shaped research across the social sciences (e.g. Georgakopoulou 2017; Marwick and boyd 2014). It also has important implications for our understanding of how online behaviour is shaped not primarily by the technology but by users' responses to their perceptions of what the technology is for, how it functions for this purpose, who they are communicating with, and the appropriate norms for doing so. This is not to dismiss the importance of technical features such as Facebook's personalisation algorithm in shaping online experiences, but rather to argue that the effect of such algorithms must always be understood in relation to how site users perceive and exploit the available affordances. If trying not to offend is a communicative dynamic shaping much Facebook use, then instances where people have been offended or have caused offence indicate the boundaries and disparities between people's different expectations, and in this way highlight the role of context design in the communicative dynamic.

ONLINE COMMUNICATION AND MEDIA IDEOLOGIES

The premise underlying this book is that Facebook, as a site for communication, is shaped in part by its users' communicative practices, and that these practices are in turn shaped by users' ideas about the context in which they are interacting. Ideologies—sets of entrenched beliefs about the social world—have long been seen as structuring people's understanding of their social realities and as justifying or interpreting their actions (see Blommaert 2005 on ideologies as they pertain to beliefs about language and discourse). These ideologies are not necessarily fixed or coherent but can be 'multiple, competing and contradictory' (Schiefflin and Doucet 1998, p. 286), as well as dynamic. Although shifting ideologies overlap and intersect, it has proved useful to separate out different types so as to more precisely pin down how they align and where they do not (Gershon 2010b, p. 284). Both language and media ideologies, for example, can be seen as subsets of people's broader sets of beliefs about semiotics. Semiotic ideologies serve to rationalise people's selection and use of signs and semiotic modes, and render them meaningful (Keane 2003). From this perspective, media ideologies are those beliefs that people have about 'the material forms people use to communicate, from bodies, phonographs, to smartphones' (Gershon 2010b, p. 283).

In exploring ideologies as they relate to Facebook, we focus primarily on media ideologies (whilst acknowledging the interplay between language and media ideologies), arguing that people's ideas about the site on which they are communicating form the basis on which they develop ideas about appropriate linguistic, communicative and behavioural norms. Our particular focus is on media ideologies as they pertain to digitally mediated platforms or channels (in the case of the research drawn upon in this book: Facebook). The proliferation of social media, Gershon (2010b, p. 290) explains, has resulted in the development of 'culturally specific, nuanced understandings of how these media shape communication and what kinds of utterances are most appropriately stated through which media'. How people reach these understandings is a subtle and varied matter which, crucially for the purposes of this book, often involves online communities implicitly negotiating and co-developing appropriate social uses (Gershon 2010c, p. 6) or, as we would also argue, learning the hard way through the experience of being judged to act inappropriately or judging others for doing so (see also Broadbent and Bauwens 2008). As this suggests, media ideologies are rarely universal, nor are they static, but instead emerge in different ways across different online communities. Despite the myriad of factors feeding into the local negotiation of people's media ideologies, it is useful to pick out three main factors which are of importance for an understanding of their influence: perceived site affordances; prior technological experience; and the place of the channel in the wider media ecology (that is, among the other opportunities for communication in the immediate digital and social environment, see, e.g. Ito et al. 2010).

The concept of affordances as applied to social media—that is, the functional opportunities that a particular platform offers to its users (Lee 2007)—is important in foregrounding the role that technologies themselves play in shaping people's ideas about how to use them. However, by claiming that a technology 'has affordances', we do not mean to suggest that its properties or features determine how somebody will act, or that all users or online communities will perceive the site functionalities in the same way. Instead, affordances emerge from a process of interaction between a particular technology and a user. It is the user who determines what they want to do with a technology and what they are able to do with it. These decisions are based on how a technology is encountered (for example, whether a platform is accessed in its web or mobile version, or which operating system is used) as well as users' critical awareness of the technology's possibilities, their prior encounters with similar technologies, their intended communicative functions, wider social patterns of technology use, and so on. As Miller and Sinanan (2014, p. 139) point out, '[o]ne reason for being cautious about concepts such as 'affordances' is that often the key elements of media usage come more from happenstance than anything that could be called the propensities of that media'. The uses of different media are often justified and explained in various ways by individuals and communities with reference to what they can or cannot do because of the technology but, Miller and Sinanan argue, these justifications are related as much to people's cultural judgements and their awareness of a site's complex and shifting functionalities (it is commonplace now for sites like Facebook to update their software on a very regular basis) than they are with what they can actually achieve with any one technology.

One outcome of this is that communities and even individuals will often use the same technology in different ways. In his study of the use of social media in an English village, for example, Miller (2016) documents the varied ways in which the villagers interpret the affordances of Twitter and thus the functions for which they use it, from the teenagers who perceive Twitter as 'personal and intimate' (p. 39) to the adults who use the site as a source of online news, one woman who uses the site to keep tabs on her abusive ex-husband, and one individual who sees it as a public platform on which to make complaints to companies. Similarly, studies of media ideologies often highlight differences in expectations between site designers and users (Barton and Lee 2013; Spitnulnik 2010). That is, media ideologies for those who use rather than design or oversee the technology can 'be at odds with the assumptions embedded in the technologies themselves' (Gershon 2010b, p. 286). One example of this can be found in Hendus's (2015) study of the 'See Translation' button on Facebook which offers machine translation of people's posts, and which, she argues, reflects Facebook's desire to overcome language barriers in its bid to make a more connected and open world (a mission that Hendus found was frequently cited by the company owners). However, certain users in her study reported not using the button in part because it was seen as violating the privacy of the sender, who may have purposefully chosen a particular language so as to address (and exclude) certain groups within their overall friend base (Hendus 2015, p. 410; see also Tagg and Seargeant 2014, for more on language choice as an addressivity strategy). In this case, users' ideas about communication on Facebook appeared to directly shape uptake of a particular affordance in ways which did not match the intentions of the designers.

People's prior experiences of technologies are central to how a current technology is perceived and exploited. Jones and Hafner (2012) note how certain social practices become associated with particular technologies to the point where it is difficult to imagine using a tool in any other way. This *technologization of practice*, as they term it, comes to influence how new technologies are exploited and evaluated; for example, people may compare social media unfavourably with more 'traditional' forms of communication because short digital posts do not seem to require the time and commitment of a handwritten letter or exploit the immediacy and directness of face-to-face interaction. Bolter and Grusin's (1999) concept of *remediation* explains how the use of new media is not only shaped by the ideologies that surround existing technologies, but how their introduction and development serves to alter the ways in which existing media are understood. For example, in her study of how people break-up using social media, Gershon (2010a) describes the fury one girl felt when her boyfriend broke up with her, not by phone, but in a handwritten letter on 'cream stationery'; 'who does that anymore?', she asked (p. 392). 'The choice of cream stationary', concludes Gershon (2010a, p. 392), 'in a context of so many other possibilities was interpreted as cold, as distancing, as disconcertingly formal'. Technology also needs to be understood in terms of the particular trajectory of the individual medium (Miller and Sinanan 2014, p. 136) so that, for example, text messaging comes to be seen as more conversational once people have mobile phone contracts and once they shift from SMS to free messaging apps such as WhatsApp (Evans and Tagg 2016). In relation to this, it is also relevant to point to the constant development of social media platforms. Facebook in particular has undergone several changes since it was opened up to the general population in 2006, not all of which have been initially popular (boyd 2008), but which tend to be eventually accepted by users and to shape subsequent behaviour, as well as people's ideas about how and why the site is used.

The more general point here is that people's perceptions of any one medium are always comparative; that is, a platform is always evaluated in relation to the other media that make up a media ecology (Horst et al. 2010) and in terms of how it finds a particular niche alongside other media. For example, within the context of how people chose to end relationships, Gershon (2010b, p. 287) suggests that decisions are shaped by students' perceptions of what is appropriate vis a vis the different options available, so that letter writing can be seen as cold in comparison to digital communication. To take an example involving Facebook, it appears that in some contexts the social network site fills a niche alongside more intimate media for sharing somewhat trivial upbeat news and keeping social acquaintances at a particular distance (Miller 2016, pp. 140–143). boyd and Marwick (2011) explain how a group of American teenagers that they surveyed switched from discussions on their (semi) public Facebook walls to more private channels—such as text messaging or what is now known as Facebook Messenger—to discuss anything 'embarrassing or upsetting, intimate or self-exposing' (p.14). As this last example illustrates, different functions within the same platform—such as status updates and Facebook Messenger—can also afford different kinds of communication.

Madianou and Miller's (2012) concept of *polymedia* is also useful in this context, in that it addresses the consequences of social and moral choice when it comes to the particular media that an individual employs, as well as their decisions to switch media (Gershon 2010a). Polymedia posits an integrated media ecology, which emerged with the recent proliferation of communication technologies but which is shaped not by a division into different platforms but in terms of cross-cutting patterns of user engagement with an 'emerging environment of communicative opportunities' (Madianou and Miller 2012, p. 170). In other words, Madianou and Miller's argument is that users should be seen not as switching between different platforms (as Gershon suggests), but as selecting more fluidly from the affordances offered across their mobile or computing device(s). We might illustrate this with the example of someone posting a photo on Instagram who might then upload it into a Facebook album, given this particular functionality afforded by Facebook (i.e. the possibility to group multiple photos together, which Instagram at present does not offer). Similarly, we might point to the example of 'crossposting' (Adami 2014) or 'transposting'—the fact that it is increasingly possible to post the same content simultaneously on different platforms—as a practice which blurs the boundaries between sites. This point is analogous to arguments in sociolinguistics regarding the use of different languages in users' communicative repertoires, while users recognise (the idea of) distinct languages and the important social and political meanings associated with them, they nonetheless often move fluidly between them in interaction in ways that suggest they are drawing on available signs in processes of 'translanguaging' rather than switching between languages (García and Li Wei 2014). Similarly, in interaction, we suggest that users might be seen as moving fluidly between platforms as they select the affordances they feel are best suited to their immediate communicative purpose.

A further argument from Madianou and Miller (2012) is that, once issues such as cost, accessibility and digital literacy skills are largely resolved (as in many, though by no means all, parts of the world), choice of media becomes ideologically significant and open to social evaluation. This has already been illustrated with the example of Gershon's break-up stories, where an individual's choice to finish a relationship by letter rather than phone is judged to be cold and distancing, while in previous contexts it was text messaging rather than direct contact which would have had this meaning. Madianou and Miller (2012, p. 180) refer to this as *resocialisation*, whereby media affordances become imbued with socially indexical meaning. Gershon's examples also make clear how digital media not only shape wider social processes (such as the break-up of a relationship) but are also shaped by them (so that which digital media are appropriate comes to be defined within the parameters of what is acceptable behaviour when it comes to breaking-up). This, as Madianou and Miller (2012, p. 174) point out, is a key tenet of theories of mediation—the representation and circulation of meaning by traditional and social media—which highlight the mutually constitutive relations between media and society (Couldry 2008; Madianou 2012; Silverstone 2002; Williams 1977). In other words, people's ideas about a particular site are not only shaped by their understanding of its affordances within the wider media ecology, but their emerging ideologies also contribute to shaping the kind of communication that takes place on it.

The starting point for our own research and for this book, then, is that Facebook users have multiple and competing ideologies about the affordances and appropriate uses of Facebook, and it is through these that they rationalise their own use of the site and justify their responses to others' actions. These ideologies are formed through negotiation (both implicit and explicit) with other users, and are shaped by users' current and past experiences with Facebook and with the technologies that preceded their use of the site, as well as by their evaluation of the social network site in comparison and in conjunction with the other platforms and channels of communication with which they engage. In line with theories of mediation, people's Facebook ideologies can be seen as both emerging from, and shaping, the wider social context; that is, how they feel about the site is not only shaped by their experiences on it but goes on to shape the nature of future experiences. By focusing on instances in which different people's ideologies do not align or are in conflict, as signalled in their reports of having been offended by others' actions or of having offended others through their own behaviour, we seek to pin down the ideological beliefs that feed into the contexts that users bring into being in this particular virtual space. In the next section we outline *Creating Facebook*, the research project that underlies this study, and the approach taken to the collection and analysis of the data.

Creating Facebook: The Research Project on Which This Book Is Based

Creating Facebook, the project around which this book is based, was a 2-year research project (2014–2016) led by Philip Seargeant and Caroline Tagg, with Amy Aisha Brown as a research fellow. The project was motivated by our previous research which drew on interactional data taken from Facebook status updates and comments to explore people's addressivity strategies and language choice (Seargeant et al. 2012; Tagg and Seargeant 2014). Whilst findings from our earlier research using interactional data highlighted who people had in mind when they styled their posts, and the impact their imagined audience had on the linguistic choices they made—issues which, as discussed above, have a fundamental influence on the nature of online communication—the interactional data left us with a number of unanswered questions regarding why people chose to post what they did, whether there were topics they purposefully avoided, and how they perceived and negotiated the dynamic norms and expectations of communication via what has become such a central part of contemporary society. *Creating Facebook*, therefore, started out as a way of exploring the motivations and perceptions that lie behind people's online behaviour, and from this developed into an investigation of the reflective understanding that people have about Facebook as a space for interaction and expression. As such it offers original insights which inform not only our own previous research, but also studies within the wider literature on language and social media which tend to rely primarily on interactional data (Georgakopoulou and Spilioti 2015; Tagg and Seargeant 2014).

The project data was collected from the online network of friends of one of the researchers, by means of two data collection instruments: an online questionnaire and follow-up interviews. The questionnaire consisted of 18 main questions (with some subdivided into multiple questions), and was designed, piloted and implemented on the online platform SurveyMonkey. In 2003, Denscombe noted that online surveys and questionnaires are not necessarily the best method of collecting data from the general population because some sections of society are less likely to be online or have the same technical skill as others, and this is likely to still hold true today, despite the growing use of Internet technology. In this instance, however, the decision was made to use an online questionnaire because the intention was to specifically target Facebook users and because it was assumed that it would be the best way of accessing the geographically diverse members of the network under investigation. In addition, this method of distributing the questionnaire through one individual's Facebook account enabled us to access the kind of (intradiverse) network that we have found typically characterises interactions on the site.

Invitations to participate in the online questionnaire were sent in mid-2014 to members of the researcher's Facebook network via personal messages on Facebook, and a link encouraging others to participate was also placed on the researcher's Facebook page. Some friends also shared the link. As Hewson and Laurent (2008, p. 67) note, this form of sampling cannot offer generalizability because it is impossible to determine the sampling frame but, as mentioned above, it does present a way of evaluating the network of interest in this study in an exploratory fashion. Of the 184 responses collected, 43 responses were discarded because they were incomplete. This left 141 responses that were subject to analysis. We describe the survey respondents in more detail in Chap. 4, when we discuss the intradiverse nature of Facebook networks.

Prior to this main survey we conducted two pilots, which gave us the opportunity to refine the research instrument, and to calibrate its focus. The original research question for these pilot projects looked at people's perceptions and awareness of the ways their posts might be viewed and interpreted by an audience *beyond* their Friends on Facebook (i.e. friends of friends, or wider), and yet the responses they elicited indicated a strong trend towards people being more concerned about how they came across to those with whom they already had an offline relationship and the issues around this (Tagg 2013). In the version of the survey used for the main project, we therefore adapted the questions to explore this in greater detail.

The questions posed in the final questionnaire were divided into two sections: the first asking for demographic details and basic information about how respondents use Facebook; the second asking questions that allowed for lengthier answers focused around what respondents do or do not post on Facebook and their rationales for and reflections on this. The overall aim of this second section was to elicit information relating to Facebook users' perceptions of their varied and potentially vast online audience, their awareness of the site affordances, their beliefs regarding their agency in exploiting these affordances, and their ideas about how all these factors influenced their linguistic and communicative practices. The specific questions we draw on in the analysis for this book comprise the following:

- Q. 14: Describe your typical status update. What do they tend to be about?
- Q. 17: Which information and/or topics would you not post about and why?
- Q. 22: Are there any instances where you have posted something which has inadvertently offended someone on Facebook? If so, please specify what it was and why it offended, and what happened as a result.
- Q. 24: Does the possibility of offending someone worry you or affect what you post on Facebook?
- Q. 26: Have you ever taken offence to something a Facebook 'friend' has posted onto Facebook? If yes, please specify what it was and why it offended, and what happened as a result.

- Q. 30: If you have ever offended or been offended, has this resulted in you changing what you write about on Facebook? If so, please specify how you have changed what you write.

For the open-ended questions, we urged respondents to 'explain [their] reasons as fully as [they] can'. Responses ranged in length, with the occasional one-word reply and a number of very lengthy answers. The survey data was used in the first instance to document the kinds of offences that took place, why and how, and how people responded to these acts of offence. As will be seen in the analysis, the responses provide evidence of context design, by highlighting users' awareness of the ways in which their identity performance and interactional behaviour online is continuously (re-)shaped in response to their interactions with other users.

Following a preliminary analysis of the questionnaire responses (see below), respondents who had given detailed responses in the questionnaire suggesting that they had either been offended or caused offence on Facebook were invited to take part in a follow-up interview. These semi-structured interviews were conducted using online voice calls, which again allowed for the opportunity to interview respondents irrespective of their physical location. The calls were recorded using QuickTime player, and the interviews were later transcribed. The interviews focused on asking the interviewees to recall and comment on times when they had caused offence and/or been offended, and some more general information about their Facebook usage and Facebook networks were also elicited.

Before completing either the online questionnaire or an interview, respondents were asked to give their consent to the use of their data in the research project. In addition, steps were taken to ensure that the participants' data was collected and stored securely. For example, SurveyMonkey enables questionnaires to be constructed on its site free of charge but that basic service does not provide the secure connection required for the collection of personal and identifying information; therefore, a more secure version was used to make sure that we could offer participants this security. Despite these steps, however, there is still the potential issue that other Facebook users may be able to access information about members of the network who participated in our project. The researcher has organised her privacy settings on Facebook so that her list of Facebook friends was private, meaning that only she can see the entire list, with other friends only being able to see common friends. However, even with this setting, Facebook offers the following warning:

> Remember: People can always see mutual friends and your friends also control who can see their friendships on their own timelines. If people can see your friendship on another timeline, theyll also be able to see it in the newsfeed, search and other places on Facebook
>
> (Facebook 2012)

We, therefore, took two main measures to protect participants. Firstly, we anonymised the questionnaire and interview responses. For the questionnaire, responses are quoted in this book without identifying participants but instead are coded for question and response number; for the interviews, we use pseudonyms. Secondly, when describing the network, reference has been made to the network as a whole or broad group therein, rather than identifying or describing individual respondents. This step is important because, as Zimmer (2010, p. 319) highlights, it is sometimes possible to identify Facebook users from information researchers supply, even in anonymised sets of data, and we saw it as essential to avoid that situation given that some of the members of the network who did not participate in the research are nonetheless mentioned in the data, and are visible to others in the network. Both steps were also seen as important because of the sensitive nature of some of the responses given by participants. Discussion of these ethical issues is essential as language research in the field develops, and feeds usefully into wider debates (Spilioti and Tagg 2016).

Our approach to the analysis of the questionnaire data, which we labelled a 'thematic-discourse analytic' approach, combined the principles and practices of both thematic analysis (Guest 2012) and discourse analysis. This approach involved two of the researchers (Philip Seargeant and Caroline Tagg) reading through the survey data and identifying key themes across the data. The two independent analyses were then compared and contrasted and a final list of themes was negotiated. The selection of themes was shaped in part by our research questions and by our focus on how users' responses to instances of offence related to their media ideologies, as well as on the current literature around relevant topics. However, we remained careful not to impose an existing framework on this new dataset but instead allow themes to emerge from the data, thus adhering to principles enshrined in a data-driven approach to data analysis. Indeed, there were a number of ways in which participants interpreted and reconstructed their online experiences, such as the importance of conflicting political views in triggering offence or the passive ways in which people claimed to respond, which we had not predicted. This approach thus enabled us to represent our respondents' voices accurately whilst remaining within the parameters of our study's aims and objectives. Importantly, the thematic analysis was accompanied throughout by discourse analysis, which involved careful consideration to the ways in which people's attitudes and perceptions were encoded linguistically. The attention to linguistic detail enabled us to take into account the importance which was discursively accorded to an issue, as well as relying on its prominence or frequency across the data. It is worth noting at this point that our study is not intended to be primarily quantitative although we have indicated frequency of themes across the data set where relevant. In this way, we identified and categorised the different stances which people discursively constructed in their answers to our survey and their perceptions of the context in which they were interacting, as well as their expression of agency in responding to their stance.

The interviews were carried out subsequent to the questionnaire, and we therefore used them to probe more deeply into the themes identified in the questionnaire data. As such, the interview data allowed for an enriched interpretation of the issues emerging from the questionnaire data, whilst also enabling us to further refine our analytic categories. In other words, we used the interview data in a data-driven fashion to include new elements or themes which entailed revisiting the questionnaire data in an iterative process which involved revising or refining our themes. For example, one issue which we explored in more detail in the interviews was that of the intersection of offline and online interactions (see Chap. 6). Whereas the questionnaire data had highlighted the way in which participants positioned Facebook interactions in a wider media ecology (e.g. as less suited than face-to-face interactions for in-depth debate), the interviews threw up the fact that people often moved between online and offline spheres in negotiating instances of offence on Facebook. Although other language and social media studies point to a blurring of the distinction between the online and offline, it is interesting that research into online abuse or aggression in this field often does not (e.g. Angouri and Tseliga 2010; Hardaker 2010) and so our research sheds light on this neglected area.

The rest of this book elaborates on and discusses the themes that emerged from our data analysis, drawing extensively on examples from our data. Before turning to the data itself, however, Chap. 2 begins by outlining our concept of context design as a key theoretical element in understanding online behaviour on social media sites such as Facebook. In Chap. 3, we then explore the literature relating to online offence, focusing on the discursive nature of online disagreement as an example of relational work, and the affordances and practices that appear to enable or encourage its occurrence on different online platforms. Following on from this explication of the academic context, we move in the next chapters to a clearer focus on our own research data. Chapters 4 and 5 explore our notion of *intradiversity* as a way of describing and explaining the nature of social networks as they are realised on Facebook. This is done in Chap. 4 by explaining how our participant sample itself represents an intradiverse network of the type we also saw evidenced in our elicited data; and, in Chap. 5, by drawing on the survey and interview data to explore the strategies that people adopt to manage their intradiverse audience, particularly when offending or taking offence, and in this way contributing to our understanding of offence as it occurs on this particular site. In Chap. 6, we draw again on our research data to explore how the management of offence is driven in part by users' desire to achieve *online conviviality* or peaceful coexistence, motivated in turn by the intradiverse characteristics of Facebook networks and shaped by the particular affordances of the site. Finally, in an Afterword to the book, we consider how our findings relate to the wider media ecology of different forms of social media, and reflect on the broader significance of our study for contemporary debates surrounding the role that Facebook and other social media sites play in political and social life, particularly the implications for understanding how online news is shared and consumed.

CHAPTER 2

Online Communication as Context Design

Abstract This chapter introduces and explains the new theoretical concept of *context design*. Our starting point is a concept central to much theorizing of online interaction: 'context collapse'—that is, the bringing together in one space of people who would not normally interact in offline contexts. This concept has been much cited in social research as a means to explore how users negotiate the management of communication in semi-public sites where they cannot fully predict the audience for their posts and so struggle to evaluate their self-presentation strategies. Although highly influential, the concept has a number of limitations, and we offer instead our own theoretical model premised on the idea that participants on Facebook imagine particularly complex contexts to which they respond as they construct their posts. We call this process *context design*, building on work in sociolinguistics which has explored the dynamic structure of spoken interaction. *Context design* examines how participants take on board a range of factors in imagining the various ways in which their online posts may be re-contextualised (embedded and reinterpreted in new contexts), and looks at how this awareness both shapes and constrains what they say.

Keywords Audience design · Context collapse · Context design · Re-contextualisation

INTRODUCING CONTEXT DESIGN

This chapter puts forward and outlines our concept of *context design* as a key dynamic in the structuring of online communication. We begin by examining the related and widely cited concept of 'context collapse'—the bringing together in one space of people who would not normally interact in offline contexts—which has been highly influential in social research for exploring how users negotiate the management of their communication in semi-public sites where they cannot fully predict the audience for their posts and so struggle to evaluate their self-presentation strategies (e.g. boyd and Marwick 2011). Despite its wide use in the literature, the concept of context collapse has largely escaped critique. The chapter provides such a critique, looking firstly at the dynamics that exist in the semi-public spaces of social media communication, and then discussing how and whether different 'contexts' can be said to collapse into one another. We go on to discuss the extent to which the affordances of a site such as Facebook allow for management of this phenomenon, how awareness of the issue is manifest in people's behaviour and what types of social implication it can have.

Having analysed the nature of communication in these terms, we go on to argue that our alternative metaphor of context design more accurately captures people's online behaviour. Building on the concept of audience design (Bell 1984), context design highlights the ways in which social media users imagine and respond to a particularly complex set of contextual variables as they design their posts and interactions. As a theoretical model, this highlights the extent to which social media encounters are shaped by a number of key factors: users' perceptions of the site they are using, theirs and others' expectations regarding appropriate behaviour and their media ideologies (see Chap. 1). Below, we illustrate these and other contextual variables through a mnemonic that sits in analogy to Hymes' (1974) SPEAKING framework. Viewing interaction in this way has important implications for our understanding of how online behaviour is shaped not primarily by the technology people are using, but by users' responses to their perceptions of what the technology is for, how it functions for this purpose, who they are communicating with and the appropriate norms for doing so.

What Is Context Collapse?

The term 'context collapse' is used to describe the phenomenon that results from the way the affordances of much social media mean that any utterance posted online can be viewed by a potentially very large and unseen audience which is likely to consist of a number of the poster's (or 'updater's') different social networks, as well as people beyond these networks—all of whom 'collapse' into a single space. The issue this raises is self-presentation, and how an individual can address simultaneously the various people that make up their online audience. As boyd (2014, p. 31) defines it, a 'context collapse occurs when people are forced to grapple simultaneously with otherwise unrelated social contexts that are rooted in different norms and seemingly demand different social responses'. This term gained currency when used by Wesch (2009) to refer to the almost limitless audience that is possible online, and the way that the different local contexts which frame an utterance all blend together. Although a similar dynamic exists to an extent in certain 'offline' social situations—e.g. weddings, where the guest list will bring together people from all different parts of a person's life; broadcast situations, where the broadcaster is addressing a large, unknown audience—because of the affordances of online communication, and in particular the fact that posts are potentially permanent and endlessly replicable (Marwick and boyd 2011), it is of particular salience for social media interaction. In short, on a site like Facebook, a user's potential audience is likely to be diverse in terms of background and values, and the precise composition of this audience for any one utterance is unknowable (boyd 2001; Marwick and boyd 2011). We discuss further the diverse nature of audiences on Facebook in Chap. 4.

One implication of these ideas about context collapse has been the development of a model of 'networked privacy' (e.g. boyd 2012; Marwick and boyd 2014). This model challenges existing ideas about privacy which focus on the individual and which rest on a binary distinction between public and private spheres (see Giaxoglou 2017). The networked nature of social media means that what one user posts can reveal as much about others as it does about themselves and also that this information can quickly circulate (boyd 2012, p. 349). In our own work, we have found that people recognise the risk of threatening the privacy of others when they post online, with one individual claiming not to post on Facebook 'Anything to do with financial issues, marital issues, anything that affects other people as much or more than me' (Tagg and Seargeant 2017). However, withholding posts is not always feasible or desirable, given the positive social capital that can be gained on social media sites like Facebook through disclosure (Ellison et al. 2011). The online situation, therefore, calls for a re-conceptualisation of privacy as a process by which people negotiate collapsed social contexts and write particular audiences into being (Marwick and boyd 2014). Marwick and boyd's ethnographic work with American teenagers reveals how young people manage the collapsed contexts of their social network accounts by adopting social or linguistic strategies that render the meaning of their posts less accessible to parents and other unintended audiences. Nissenbaum (2010) draws attention to the importance of a contextual approach to determining the 'informational norms'—norms surrounding what information is shared, how and with whom—in a particular online space. In Marwick and boyd's (2014) case, the American teenagers could be seen as reinforcing local social norms about the intended privacy of their technically public posts. Similarly, in her study of the publically available parenting forum Mumsnet, Mackenzie (2017) shows how users assume an audience of like-minded users, despite the potentially infinite audience that could gain access to their posts. Such research highlights the significant role that the notion of context collapse has played in redefining our understanding of online social practices.

The importance of the notion of context collapse for an understanding of online interaction within sociolinguistics lies in the fact that people typically adjust their style and content according to their understanding of who they are talking to, and thus complex notions of audience result in potentially complex dynamics of communication. Bell's (1984) framework of 'audience design' is useful in theorising these dynamics. The framework was initially developed to explain why one newsreader would vary their pronunciation when reading the news on a different radio station, which he felt was due to their having imagined a different audience. At the time, studies of speaker style were dominated by Labov's seminal insights into how stylistic variation depended on the degree of attention a speaker paid to their own speech, and Bell's research helped to propel the importance of audience to the foreground. This is not to say that Bell was the first to explore this line of thinking, and his framework draws on Bakhtin's (1930s/1981) ideas about addressivity—the ways in which meaning is shaped by both the speaker and the addressee—and on other interactional frameworks which drew attention to the importance of audience in shaping speaker style (Clark and Carlson 1982; Garfinkel 1967; Goffman 1981; Sacks et al. 1974), whilst also having parallels with speech accommodation theory (Giles and Powesland 1975) and its focus on how speakers converge with, or diverge from, other interlocutors.

In short, audience design holds that the stylistic choices made by a speaker are shaped in part by their consideration of, and accommodation to, the varied segments that make up their audience (Bell 1984). The addressee (the person or people being directly addressed) will have most influence over speaker style, but style will also be shaped by others present in the exchange, including auditors (others whose presence in the exchange is ratified by the speaker) and overhearers (those who are present but whose presence is not ratified). The specific nature of people's relationships is important in determining the impact of these individuals on speaker style, so that in Youssef (1993) study, a child uses standard forms whenever her mother is present, regardless of who the child is addressing. Generally, however, audience design posits that people's influence on speaker style is determined by how they are positioned in the immediate exchange by the speaker. This aspect of the framework—the active positioning of others by the speaker—goes some way to address the criticism made by other researchers (e.g. Finegan and Biber 2001) that the framework is overly 'responsive' in that speakers are seen as reacting to predetermined audiences. The fact that roles are not predetermined but allocated by the speaker is particularly relevant for online situations such as Facebook in which the audience is 'invisible' (Litt 2012) and must be imagined into being; that is, where speakers construct their intended audience through their stylistic choices.

Also relevant in this regard is Bell's (1999, 2001) subsequent development of ideas about 'initiative style shift'. According to these ideas, as well as responding to an imagined audience, speakers may also accommodate to absent third parties, to which the speaker may or may not belong. These acts of accommodation involve what Bell called initiative style shifts in that they do not simply respond to the situation at hand but serve to shape it by drawing on and making relevant other contexts. Responsive and initiative style shifts can be seen as 'two complementary and coexistent dimensions of style' (Bell 2001, p. 165). In virtual situations, however, the distinction between these two kinds of style shifting is blurred, both by the varied and invisible nature of the audience (which, as mentioned above and argued by boyd 2001, requires users to create a new audience for every post) and by the emergent nature of norms on sites such as Facebook (McLaughlin and Vitak 2011), which encourage users to take the initiative in shaping the online space and determining communicative norms.

As suggested above, the basic principle of audience design also holds for online contexts. However, the particular affordances of communication via social network sites (SNSs) are likely to result in interesting differences between the type of audiences perceived by someone posting on an SNS such as Facebook, and the audiences which Bell's model describes for spoken interaction. Firstly, unlike either conversational or broadcast talk, the type of interactions that typically take place on SNSs are conducted via the written mode and can, therefore, be edited and planned, and yet at the same time they exhibit much of the interactivity and informality that is often found in speech (As a side note, the extent to which the written mode dominates may be shifting, as voice and video messaging appear to becoming increasingly popular on services such as WhatsApp and WeChat). Secondly, to the extent that posts can, therefore, range somewhere along a cline between personal conversation and public broadcasts, SNSs can be described as 'semi-public' forums in the sense that a user's audience, while often large, diverse and unseen, generally comprises people they know. In earlier work on audience design on Facebook (Tagg 2013; Tagg and Seargeant 2014), we found that posts were shaped by users' awareness not only of an active circle of Friends likely to respond to their post but also a wider circle of Friends—distant relatives, old school friends, friends of friends—who may also gain access to their posts. Posters managed this aspect of context collapse by drawing on a range of linguistic and communicative strategies to mark their utterances as public or private, including language choice and code-switching, vague language and contextualised reference. This work, along with other studies (Frobenius 2014; Page 2014a; Johnson 2013), shows how a recognition of context collapse forms the starting point for the development of models of online audience design which begin to explain how social media users manage the complex contexts in which they operate.

As the above suggests, the sociolinguistic concept of audience design enables a more nuanced understanding of how context collapse is negotiated through language. Audience design is a more dynamic view of communication than that offered by context collapse, but it remains limited by its focus on 'audience' as the key contextual variable, especially given that the 'audience' is being addressed in a different 'context' to that in which they might meet offline. It does not easily explain how people's ideas about their 'audience' emerge both from past offline communication histories with others and also from their perception of the immediate social media context nor does it account for the impact of people's awareness of the future trajectories of their posts on their language choices.

WHY RE-EXAMINE CONTEXT COLLAPSE?

While the concept of context collapse has been very useful in highlighting this general issue of the broad and complex nature of the online audience for social media postings, and the way in which this phenomenon is more salient in online than offline communication, it is nevertheless a rather blunt tool for a fine-grained analysis of online interaction. For this reason, we go on below to deconstruct the notion and analyse the elements of the phenomenon in closer detail.

A key issue in this respect lies in the understanding of 'context' which underpins the metaphor of collapse. In particular, the metaphor presupposes a notion of context as a somewhat fixed set of situational factors which exist independently of what Duranti and Goodwin (1992, p. 3) call the 'focal event' or the 'phenomenon being contextualised': for sociolinguists, the focal event is likely to be an act of spoken or written communication often referred to as a 'text'. (The concept of 'text' here refers to any specific occurrence of language and communication—e.g. a Facebook post, email, a transcribed conversation which can be either spoken, written, or include multi-modal elements.) For contexts to collapse, they must not only have an independent existence but be conceived of as discrete entities, demarcated from the other contexts into which they collapse. There is also an implied assumption that when a person comes online, they bring an offline context with them—they reproduce the offline context online—a view which obscures the other variables which influence context, not the least of which is what Halliday and Hasan (1976) labelled 'Mode'—the type of medium or channel of communication—so that the context for any online post is shaped not only by who is being addressed but by the particular platform (e.g. Facebook) and channel (e.g. status updating rather than messaging) being used.

Sociolinguistics—as with other linguistics and social science fields—has witnessed a shift over the last century away from a model of context as a relatively fixed social and cultural setting against which an utterance must be interpreted (Malinowski 1923) and towards a vision of context as a dynamic construct collaboratively brought into being through interaction (Duranti and Goodwin 1992). This understanding of context has implications for the validity and usefulness of the concept of context collapse as a way of understanding how people manage online communications. In this section, therefore, we briefly elaborate on how context has been conceptualised in sociolinguistics, both in consideration of offline and, more recently, online interactions. In doing so, we highlight the value that sociolinguistic insights can bring to a scholarly understanding of social media.

Sociolinguistic Understandings of Context

Defining 'Context'

The concept of 'context' has been used in language analysis in at least two distinct ways (Crystal 2003, pp. 108–109). Firstly, it can be used as a synonym of 'co-text' to refer to the wider text in which a linguistic feature is used (the 'linguistic context'). This is the context referred to by corpus linguists who look at 'key words in context' (KWIC) and who have found that meaning resides not in a word but in wider phrases (Hunston 2002). It is also the primary focus for discourse analysts who look at language 'beyond the sentence'; that is, the role of coherence and cohesion in creating a socially meaningful text (Cook 1989, p. 7). The second use of 'context' refers to features and phenomenon beyond the text—i.e. the 'social context' or situation including (for example) the participants, their relationships to each other, the type of interaction they are engaging in and the medium being used. The social and linguistic ethnographer Bronislaw Malinowski (1923) is often credited with highlighting the importance of language in context as a way of interpreting the cultural practices of groups and the way that these are rendered meaningful within the culture and environment in which they take place. In this book, we focus particularly on this second conceptualisation of context, and how it has been developed by linguistic ethnographers and sociolinguists, among others.

It is worth pointing out however that, despite the distinct uses that have been made of co-text and context, it is not necessarily always possible or desirable to distinguish the text (language and its co-text) from its context. For example, texts or stretches of talk themselves can be seen as contextualising other texts or stretches of talk (Goodwin and Duranti 1992). In his study of verse within a story, Bauman (1992) shows how the narration of the story is at once contextualised by the surrounding speech events and provides a context within which the verse is understood. Distinguishing between text, co-text and context is arguably particularly challenging for researchers of online discourse. As Crystal (2011) points out, online texts may be particularly fluid and dynamic and their boundaries hard to define. For example, Crystal asks whether a 'text' constitutes one forum message or extends to the entire, continuously growing thread, as well as the other elements visible on the screen (including those generated by the site and those contributed by advertisers) and any hyperlinked texts. In the case of Facebook, this is further complicated by the different platforms via which the site can be used (phone, tablet, PC), each of which has a different physical layout and format.

As well as questions as to where 'context' ends and 'co-text' begins, there is a lack of agreement about the outer limits of context, and an acknowledgement that not all aspects of context can be available to a researcher (Ochs 1979, p. 2). As Cook (1990, p. 5) concludes in an article entitled 'Transcribing infinity', capturing all relevant contextual variables is a 'theoretical as well as a practical impossibility'. It is this complex, ambiguous and potentially infinite understanding of context which underlies our investigation of how context is perceived, co-constructed and responded to on Facebook.

Mapping the Social

Researchers of language in context initially assumed a systematic set of relations between language and context, which results in predictable patterns in language use according to its context. From a Hallidayan perspective, for example, the 'context of situation' is inscribed into, and therefore can be retrieved from, the text:

> the context of situation, the context in which the text unfolds, is encapsulated in the text, not in a kind of piecemeal fashion, not at the other

extreme in any mechanical way, but through a systematic relationship between the social environment on the one hand, and the functional organisation of language on the other.

(Halliday and Hasan 1985, p. 11)

Whilst usefully systematising the link between language and context, the assumption that analysts can reconstruct context from a text neglects consideration of how context is attended to and manipulated by participants as an interaction unfolds (Goodwin and Duranti 1992, p. 9). Dell Hymes' work has been especially important for laying out a set of descriptive constructs for a perspective on context that starts not with the text but with the *social*. Hymes (1972) replaced a grammatical approach based on units of analysis such as sentence, clause and phrase with a socially oriented approach centred around units of analysis such as speech community, speech event and speech act, all of which comprise linguistic and non-linguistic features and are governed not only by 'rules of speaking' but by other social conventions (Cameron 2001, p. 55). Although there have been a number of different attempts to map the contextual features that shape language use (e.g. Ochs 1979), the most comprehensive and widely known is probably Hymes' (1974) SPEAKING mnemonic. This framework details the contextual variables that make up speech events such as conversations or speeches.

S   Setting: that is, where the speech event is located in time and space, as distinct from the 'scene', which is the 'psychological setting' or the 'cultural definition of an occasion' (Hymes 1977, p. 18). Setting is analogous to 'physical' and 'social' spaces;
P   Participants: the people who take part in the speech event, and their role in this (e.g. speaker, addressee, audience, eavesdropper);
E   Ends: that is, what the purpose of the speech event is, and what its outcome is meant to be, from community and individual viewpoints (e.g. to entertain, to chastise, to instruct);
A   Act sequence: the speech acts that make up the speech event (e.g. general question followed by response; speech followed by congratulations), as well as message form and content;
K   Key: the tone or manner of performance (e.g. serious or joking, sincere or ironic)—analogous to Goffman's 'social frames' or footings;
I   Instrumentalities: the channel or medium of communication being used (e.g. speaking, signing, writing, typing) and what language, variety, style or register is selected from the participants' repertoires;

N   Norms of interaction and interpretation: what the rules are for producing and interpreting speech acts and the 'specific behaviours and properties that attach' (Hymes 1977, p. 20);
G   Genres: that is, what socially recognised 'type' does a speech event belong to, or what genres are drawn on in a speaker's utterance

(Hymes 1977; see also Cameron 2001, p. 56; Farah 1998, p. 126)

Although Hymes' model of contextual variables facilitates systematic analysis of a speech event, this is not to say that it is necessarily applicable to all social situations nor does it provide insight into the wider social or cultural significance of a particular event (Cameron 2001). As we shall see, however, the model proves useful in isolating the different aspects of context that people must attend to when designing the particular context for an online post, and below we put forward our own mnemonic for better understanding online communication in the light of our ideas about context design.

From Style to Stylisation

Meanwhile, William Labov's pioneering work (Labov 1966) had spearheaded the formation of a new field of study: variationist sociolinguistics, or what has since been termed 'First wave variation studies' (Eckert 2012). The field came to be characterised by the use of quantitative methods through which broad correlations between linguistic patterning and wider social structures could be made (Labov 1972; Trudgill 1974). This work succeeded in confirming and detailing the systematic and socioeconomically stratified nature of linguistic variability. However, the focus on pre-existing macrosocial categories (e.g. age, gender, nationality) relegated people to 'bundles of demographic characteristics' (Eckert 2012, p. 88). This limitation was addressed to some extent by the second wave of variation studies, which adopted ethnographic methods in order to explore how people position themselves in relation to macrosocial categories. But whilst avoiding the abstract conception of context used in the first wave, studies continued to explain linguistic patterns as a *product* of social context (Eckert 2012). It was not until the third wave, in the twenty-first century, that researchers began exploring language variation as emerging from people's dynamic enactment of speaking styles (Coupland 2014; Podesva 2007). As Eckert (2012, p. 98) concludes, '[i]t has become clear that patterns of variation do not simply unfold from the speaker's structural position in a system of production, but are part of the active—stylistic—production of social differentiation', which has implications for an understanding of the symbiotic relationship between style and context.

Interactional sociolinguistics, and in particular the work of John Gumperz (e.g. 1982), can be seen as instrumental in initialising this re-conceptualisation of the notion of context (Verscheuren 2010, p. 171). Through his ethnographic research, Gumperz challenged the validity of generalised and abstracted notions of context, as well as the assumption that straightforward correlations could be made between speech communities and linguistic features. Instead, he showed that language use was shaped by people's perceptions of the relationships between linguistic forms and social realities, and that these could only be understood through situated, ethnographic investigation of unfolding interactions: what he referred to as an 'ethnography of communication' (Gumperz and Hymes 1972). He observed how certain features—particularly prosody—are drawn upon to signal to interlocutors how an exchange is to be interpreted; in other words, they are used as a means of contextualising an utterance. To adopt Goffman's terminology, these features signal the social framing (i.e. the way of organising social experience) of an utterance, which offers expectations about how it should be understood. In addition, they can also indicate a change in how an utterance should be interpreted; what Goffman calls a shift in footing or 'a change in the alignment we take to ourselves and the others present' (Goffman 1981, p. 128). Importantly, these 'contextualisation cues', as Gumperz calls them [and which he glosses as 'any feature of linguistic form that contributes to the signalling of contextual presuppositions' (Gumperz 1967, p. 131)], are not pre-existing or pre-determined associations between context and language, but themselves emerge as part of and contribute to the interactive construction of context.

Like most linguistic anthropology of the time, Gumperz's work drew on spoken interactions and he, therefore, drew attention to the role of prosodic markers as contextualisation cues. In her later study of Greek emails, Georgakopoulou (1997) shows that contextualisation cues are relevant not only in spoken interactions and synchronous online chat but also in asynchronously exchanged online messages. She shows how, in the absence of verbal cues, participants drew on 'code-centred contextualisation cues' (p. 149) which, for the multilingual email writers in her study, often took the form of code-switching as well as style-shifting. Through switches between standard Greek, local Greek dialects and English, the writers constructed 'a multivoiced and pastiche style' which 'forms the context within which activities on email can and should be interpreted' for that community of friends (Georgakopoulou 1997, p. 147). Below we take a wider look at how the dynamic, socially constructed understanding of context has shaped research into online settings.

Context Online

A number of assumptions relevant to context appear to underlie early research into social exchanges via the Internet: that a distinction could be made between the online and offline worlds; that online communication was 'bodiless' (Hall 1996; Sutton 1999) and decontextualised (Meyrowitz 1985); and that existing social contexts and identities are irrelevant online (Turkle 1995). Technological and social changes, as well as developments in the way online discourse is theorised, challenge these assumptions, showing firstly that people's existing social roles—as parent, family member, employee—can remain very relevant online (Tagg and Seargeant 2017) as can social categories such as gender (Newon 2011). Secondly, it has become evident that online activities should increasingly be seen as an extension of what an individual or group is doing offline (see, for example, Monaghan 2014). As Jurgenson (2012) argues, the fact that we are often 'online' shapes our perception of the world when we are 'offline' (for example, we might use Google to resolve a face-to-face debate), just as we never leave behind the 'offline' when we go 'online'. Mobile devices, in particular, are seen as enabling processes of multitasking which extend across online and offline environments (Cohen 2015; Lyons and Tagg in preparation). This everyday blurring of online–offline boundaries was strikingly reflected in the highly publicised release in July 2016 of Pokémon Go, an augmented reality game which required players to find and target virtual creatures in real-world locations, often with alarming consequences [e.g. people getting into car accidents while playing the game while driving (Mullen 2016)]. Increasingly, therefore, rather than seeing virtual interactions as being decontextualised and divorced from 'real life', researchers are now recognising the apparent richness and complexity of context in online interaction.

Far from being decontextualised, then, digitally mediated interactions are seen more and more as involving the careful negotiation of multiple contexts and thus particularly complex processes of 'contextualisation work' (Androutsopoulos 2014, p. 6), that is, the active construction and negotiation of context as part of the communicative exchange. According to Moore (2004), online interactions involve a 'doubling of place' in the sense that digitally mediated communication makes relevant a virtual as well as a physical context. Jones (2009) shows how people transfer their attention between a number of different virtual and physical spaces as they carry out social and communicative activities. He describes, for example, how posing for, taking and looking at photos is at once part of a night out for young Hong Kongers, whilst simultaneously a way of engaging with a virtual community (and see also Lyons 2014, who draws attention to the discursive strategies people use in co-constructing a shared online space, including the discursive enactment of physical actions).

The relative lack of access to social cues in social media contexts—accent, gender, age, tone of voice, facial expression, gesture—does not render offline contexts irrelevant, but it does mean that interlocutors must recreate or exploit offline contexts through the resources available online in order to co-construct a shared online context which shapes interpretations of their posts. In boyd's (2001, p. 119) words, social media participants engage in *writing* themselves into being. That is, their postings are contextualised not through physical co-presence but through the use of largely visual and often text-based resources—spelling, punctuation, font, emoticons, emoji, stickers, photos and so on. Their understanding of context is not individual but social or 'networked'; as Marwick and boyd (2014, p. 1058) point out, users 'must understand how others have shaped the context and operate accordingly', and in this way reproduce and maintain the context. The importance of this contextualisation work for the issues dealt with in this book lies in the agency which it implies users have in shaping online contexts. In Androutsopoulos's (2014, p. 17) words, the implication is that online context is 'not just delimited by technological means but construed by speakers and audiences'.

Despite this growing body of work on the topic, much of the relevant literature remains limited to one-to-one interactions through relatively private channels, such as chat rooms and text messaging (e.g. Jones 2004,

2009; Lyons 2014). Status updating on a semi-public site like Facebook, which is our focus here, is likely to be particularly complex in this respect. Firstly, as boyd (2001) points out, given the potentially wide yet invisible audience on Facebook, updaters cannot be certain as to who will read their posts and thus they must engage in constructing the various contexts in which they envisage their posting be read. Secondly, as well as generating new contexts for an update, updaters must also contend with the awareness that unintended 'overhearers' may be listening (i.e. those people who have access to their posts by, for example, being friends of friends), and thus adopt complex audience design strategies aimed at targeting some individuals and excluding others (Tagg and Seargeant 2014), which again requires a nuanced understanding of contextual variables.

And finally, the possibility of entextualisation (Bauman and Briggs 1990, p. 73)—the detachment of a text from its original setting and its re-contextualisation elsewhere—is particularly salient in semi-public, networked environments like Facebook. Androutsopoulos (2014) theorises online entextualisation in terms of 'sharing', a process which involves selecting posts, styling them and negotiating with others. Sharing a post as an act of entextualisation is also an act of transformation which imbues the original post with personal or social significance and thus creates 'significant moments for a networked audience' (p. 4). As Androutsopoulos (2014) argues, the act of sharing—of '[u]nderstanding such moments and participating in their interactive negotiation' (p. 6)—presupposes a great deal of shared background knowledge and user alignment. Nonetheless, as far as the original poster is concerned, posts that are shared or remixed will appear in new contexts which make them available to unanticipated users and which frame these posts in different ways, leading to new interpretations. In our *Creating Facebook* research, we have found that people often try to guess the possible future trajectories of their posts, and that this contextualisation work often shapes what and how they post (Tagg and Seargeant 2017). We return to these three points—the unknown audience, the existence of overhearers and the possibility of entextualisation—later in this chapter.

Summary: A Sociolinguistic Perspective on Context Collapse

Bringing this all together, the question we seek to answer in this book is whether the concept of context collapse can account for a model of context as actively co-constructed by users in the course of their online interactions; and, if not, how these online processes can best be conceptualised. On the one hand, the metaphor is a striking one which to some extent has transcended its metaphorical connotations to stand for a shortcut for the kinds of situations generated in online spaces such as Facebook, and in this sense is useful for discussions of networked privacy and audience design. On the other hand, our discussion so far points to limitations to the concept in terms of the extent to which it accurately models what happens when people interact—both offline and online.

The main issue is that as a metaphor it rests on the assumption that, on online sites such as Facebook, various offline contexts are reproduced in one virtual space. The metaphor thus relies on a problematic understanding of 'context' as being discrete, fixed and pre-existing. This understanding sits in contrast to sociolinguistic understandings of context. Sociolinguists, as we have seen, would say that contexts continually shift that one utterance sets the context for the next, that people interact in a dynamic fashion which reshapes their perceptions and so the contextual frame in which interlocutors use to give meaning to their utterances continuously shifts. Contexts, according to this interpretation, do not exist independently of a text and nor are they 'countable' as implied by the metaphor. Another assumption implied by the metaphor is that offline contexts can collapse into, and coexist within, one online space. This assumption rests on the understanding that offline contexts can be reproduced online, specifically through the individuals (the Facebook Friends) which a user associates with a particular context. This understanding can be challenged on at least two fronts. Firstly, it foregrounds audience as the key aspect of context at the expense of other contextual variables, such as those highlighted by Hymes (1974). Hymes, neglecting among other things to consider the impact that the change of mode (the shift in medium) might engender when people move online to Facebook. Secondly, it assumes that any one of a user's Facebook Friends represents—and involves the user responding to—a particular offline context, when in reality people's offline lives are likely more complex than that implies.

As well as assuming that offline contexts are reproduced online, the metaphor also rests on the assumption that these contexts then coexist as discrete entities which a user may or may not attend to. From a sociolinguistic perspective, it is not so much that these contexts continue to exist online, but that features of their offline realisations remain available to speakers ('updaters' or 'posters') as potential influences on their stylistic choices. In that sense, offline contexts do not pre-exist in this online space, but are made relevant through (to borrow Bell's term) the updater's initiative style shifts. This is in effect where audience design comes in, because Bell's (and others') point is that people do not respond to a pre-existing audience but construct an idea of the audience through how they design their interactions. How people perceive the audience is based on what they know about it and what they understand the consequences of the audience are for how they should come across. What we are suggesting, by drawing on a sociolinguistics understanding of context, is that the styling of an utterance involves far more than a concern for audience, but the imagining and reproduction of much fuller relevant scenarios; by responding to how you think your mother might react to what you say, you are bringing into play a long-term communication history, social ideologies as they relate to parenthood, the various domestic and social settings that make up your relationship and so on. In other words, the process of choosing how to style an utterance brings in many other dimensions alongside audience.

Given the complexity of the typical Facebook network, updaters likely orient towards what Blommaert (2010) refers to as multiple centres of influence as they actively construct a context for a particular posting. Facebook, like other online sites, can thus be seen a 'polycentric' space in which people attend simultaneously to a number of coexisting, often competing, orientations which can include traditional sources of authority, peer group norms or 'abstract entities and ideas' (Blommaert 2010, p. 39) all of which cut across traditionally perceived offline (and online) contexts. As Androutsopoulos and Staehr (2017) point out, however, research into social media has tended to neglect consideration of the polycentricity of online interactions or to take into account the fluidity of online and offline norms and the ways in which resources and normative centres are entextualised and taken up across online sites. Our re-conceptualisation of context collapse in terms of polycentricity moves us away from a responsive or reactive model which assumes distinctions between the online and offline text and context, towards a model which recognises the active way in which users work to co-construct an online context shaped by their awareness of centres of normativity and their shifting orientation towards them. In the next section, we develop this further as we elaborate on our concept of 'context design'.

Context Design: A Refined Model

Our concept of context design takes into account the fluid, socially co-constructed nature of context in order to better understand the communicative dynamics that shape social media encounters. In processes of context design, we argue, people shape their utterances in response to the various centres of influence which they feel are likely to determine how their utterances are interpreted by different members or segments of their intended or possible audience. In other words, they design a context for each utterance which draws on, sustains and extends existing sources of authority regarding what is deemed appropriate or valued behaviour. Crucial to this process is the argument that people are not responding to a complete pre-existing social setting but that, in styling an utterance, they are involved in actively constructing the context or frame in which it will or can be interpreted.

When updating status on Facebook, users must typically take into account what is usually a particularly complex set of contextual considerations, given the invisible but potentially intradiverse nature of their potential audience and thus the various, often competing and overlapping centres of influence towards which orient. In relation to this, a number of researchers have pointed to the increased likelihood for self-reflexivity given the conditions in which online posts are composed (Deumert 2014; Tagg 2016). According to Androutsopoulos and Staehr (2017), reflexivity is heightened by the 'temporal gap between composition and release'; that is, opportunities for engaging in processes of context design are made available in the time the poster has between composing a message and transmitting it (hitting send) as well as the fact that posts can be revisited and scrutinised after they are sent. Online reflexivity is also likely to be enhanced as a result of the feedback which online posters on a site like Facebook receive from their intradiverse audience when they are forced to consider, through exposure to conflicting perspectives, their own views. This may be part of a more general trend in contemporary conditions of globalisation; as Coupland (2003) argues, new diversities and mobilities are serving to shake people's assumptions about social relations in ways that increase reflexive behaviour. On Facebook, this feedback loop is enforced by the way users are encouraged by site design decisions to reflect on, and respond to, others' posts through 'liking' them or commenting on them (Androutsopoulous and Staehr 2017). This observation lies at the heart of context design:

the way in which users respond to previous experiences on the site when styling future posts. To return to the main point above then, processes of context design, which are also part of the process of targeting and styling spoken utterances, may be somewhat more conscious, elaborate and potentially problematic in online situations, given the inherently reflexive property of online writing and the nature of invisible, intradiverse online audiences.

Models of audience design such as Bell's (and these models' application to online situations) take into account the constructed nature of audience but, by focusing on this as their central concept, they neglect the other contextual elements to which speakers and online users must attend. An individual's understanding of their audience includes their awareness of, for example, the personal network of each audience member, the wider social and cultural norms to which they ascribe, and the situations that may arise if they do not address them appropriately. Building on existing frameworks for spoken interactions such as Hymes, we argue that Facebook users must, primarily, take into account the following elements when styling a post and designing the context in which it is intended to be understood. Below, we organise the elements within the mnemonic of POSTING, in analogy with Hymes' (1974) SPEAKING framework [note: Thanks to Korina Giaxoglou for suggesting this mnemonic].

P Participants: the context constructed in a post is shaped by the poster's general knowledge of the people they are friends with and their experience of their past behaviour and interaction on the site, as well as the more immediately relevant feedback provided by their interlocutors' responses to their posts. As soon as someone comments on a status update, for example, the status updater is more likely to orient to them and their likely expectations in ensuing posts, be these either comments in the same thread or subsequent updates. As we explain in Tagg and Seargeant (2014), people whom a user sees as 'active Friends'—those who can be expected to reply, based on past behaviour—are likely to have a greater influence over the stylisation of a post than those who tend not to reply or about whom the node user has only a vague awareness. Importantly, the more immediately relevant feedback provided by a reply does not make the intended audience any more 'real', but rather we can describe the imagined audience as being more or less 'grounded' in relevant evidence.

O   Online media ideologies: as discussed in Chap. 1, people's ideas about the purpose of Facebook in relation to other platforms, and how status updating works in relation to other channels on Facebook, shape the kind of post they will contribute to the site.
S   Site affordances: awareness of, and attitudes towards, affordances, both of the site itself and online texts more generally. As discussed above, affordances are also socially constructed; it is not simply the case that Facebook 'has' affordances which people either do or do not recognise. Rather, they are the product of people's awareness and use of potential site functionalities.
T   Text type (or mode) in which the communication takes place. That is to say, the fact that online communication is often typed, includes the ability to use visual resources, and is characterised by physical distance, quasi-synchronicity and networked resources.
I   Identification processes: as Leppänen et al. (2014) argue, the performative co-construction of 'self' is a key element of online interaction. When posting, users are not only taking into account external or 'other' centres of influence but are actively involved in positioning themselves in relation to existing norms—(dis)aligning themselves with particular ideologies, discourses and individuals, as well as attaching themselves to, or distancing themselves from, ascribed social roles (Tagg and Seargeant forthcoming). Thus, context design also involves an awareness of self and of the ways in which an individual wishes to perform and make visible their identity, commonality, connectedness and belonging (see also Leppänen et al. 2017).
N   Norms of communication: these will vary between groups at different scales of interaction (Blommaert 2010). On a higher scale, interaction on Facebook will be shaped by widely circulating cultural, religious and political beliefs and values, such as the reverence accorded to the monarchy in some countries, adherence to a liberal doctrine or ideas about what constitutes racist or sexist behaviour. On a lower scale of interaction, local peer norms regarding appropriate behaviour between friends and how Facebook should be used, for example, will extend between offline and online spaces but will also be to some extent platform-specific or related to communication on a particular site (i.e. shaped by the affordances of Facebook and the purposes to which it is put). In certain cases, norms could include specific regulations as a result of policies laid down by the site company, such as the prohibitions on Facebook

against nudity, as interpreted and negotiated by particular user groups and, often, imposed by legal regulations. These multiple, often conflicting centres of influence sit at the heart of our analysis of acts of offence.
G   Goals or immediate purposes or ends when posting. So, for example, one might be making a joke or being ironic, in which case it is necessary to signal this in order to create the context in which your post can be interpreted. This role may be fulfilled by contextualisation cues such as emoji and emoticons.

Our argument, then, is that on Facebook users have a semi-conscious awareness of these elements (as well as other less-prominent elements) in relation to how their posts are likely to be received and interpreted, and that this awareness influences their behaviour on the site.

As well as attending to these elements of the polycentric space when designing the context in which their postings are interpreted, we argue that Facebook users also take into account the trajectory or multiple trajectories along which their posts might travel. The notion of a text's trajectory (Blommaert 2005) allows for the fact that texts do not exist solely in their original context but that they move around by being reproduced and reinterpreted in new contexts. As originating in Bauman and Briggs' (1990) work, this process of entextualisation—the lifting or 'decontextualising' of a text from one context to be 'recontextualised' in another—can involve transformations in the meaning of a text or language resource and in the value accorded to it. For example, a comment made by a politician during a debate may be removed from that context and re-appropriated as a meme by those opposing that politician. The words will remain precisely the same, but the meaning, by dint of the way these words are re-contextualised, is quite different. On Facebook, users may attend to the likelihood of entextualisation through online sharing (Androutsopoulos 2014) that selected posts will appear in numerous newsfeeds, including those of Friends of Friends and that they may be restyled or reframed during their trajectories by the nature of the comments they attract and by the posts they appear alongside (that is, what Androutsopoulos calls 'negotiation'). A post could also be interpreted (without being reused) in a different context—e.g. by a child looking at his father's newsfeed. Previous research has explored the way in which even private digitally mediated communication between two persons makes relevant multiple spaces—the virtual space, multiple physical spaces (e.g. Jones 2004)—but our approach highlights the increase in complexity engendered by the conditions of online social networking, brought about not only by the large, intradiverse audience but also by largely unpredictable processes of online sharing or entextualisation. Facebook users must potentially attend to an almost infinite array of communicative spaces that may be made relevant through intradiversity and entextualisation.

In seeking to understand this complexity, we identify the main 'stages' of the text trajectory that a user may attend to when writing a post as likely to include the following:

- The longer communicative histories between a user and members of their Friends network. How a post is stylised on a social network site like Facebook is likely to be grounded in the posters' awareness of their existing and habitual relationships with individual friends and friend groups, including the norms and values the posters assume these friends to have, their shared background knowledge, existing communication history and the posters' understanding of the potential offline implications of their post, which can range from upsetting someone to losing their job. Posts thus draw on, extend and transform longer term patterns of interaction.
- The immediate online setting of Facebook. This is defined by the speaker's understanding of Facebook and of the different people who make up their friends as well as their understanding of how this intradiversity can be managed (i.e. through built-in affordances or linguistic strategies).
- Imagined future trajectories of posts. This is based on an understanding of relationships which are dynamic and which exist in time (e.g. posts persist, they can be re-posted, your Friends list may grow, privacy settings may be changed—all of which means that people at some unanticipated future date may look at and interpret what you have written). Our research in this area suggests that people can be constrained in what they post by the feeling that they lack control over the future trajectory of their posts—a phenomenon which we have called 'fear of extextualistion' [note: Thanks to Adrienne Lo for suggesting this term] and which involves awareness that their posts may be interpreted differently if or when they are re-contextualised.

A final, crucial element of context design lies in the extent to which people navigate and manage the multiple centres of influence to which they variously orient. How context is designed depends on people's awareness of the competing norms and sources of authority, but also on their sense of agency in acting on this awareness. This relates to the linguistic and communicative strategies they are able to implement in achieving their interactional aims, the resources they have available and what they choose to or can do with them and the extent to which they feel they can exploit the site affordances. Users' agency will be constrained in various ways not only by their awareness of what is available and their access to resources, but by their social roles and how they are positioned by others. Focusing on the strategies available to users, and what users have to say about them, is a key aspect of the methodology involved in investigating the construction of context.

Conclusion

In sum, the premise of our theoretical model is that participants on Facebook imagine particularly complex contexts to which they respond as they construct their posts, a process which we call 'context design'. Although context design is a feature of all interaction, it is of specific note online—at least in written interactions—due to the increased likelihood for reflexivity and by the particular nature of the typical online audience for postings on sites such as Facebook. The concept examines how participants can take on board a range of factors in imagining the various ways in which their online posts may be re-contextualised (embedded and reinterpreted in new contexts) and looks at how this awareness shapes and constrains what they say as they construct the contexts in which they wish their posts to be interpreted. It thus draws on a sociolinguistic understanding of context as co-constructed as well as on audience design models which draw attention to the way in which elements of context are co-constructed through stylisation in order to explain the communicative dynamics shaping interactions. As one of our interviewees, Jacob, sums up the implications of context design:

(2)   I think that the topics that are chosen actually end up shaping what Facebook is for many people. So I think in certain groups of people, choosing to talk about different topics, that becomes their Facebook experience.

[Jacob, interview]

In other words, Facebook, as a space for communication, is shaped by how its users decide to use it. Their decisions about what to post create a particular user experience, which then goes on to shape future contributions to the site. As we discuss later, this then has implications for our understanding of the relationship between technology and society, and in particular the extent to which online technologies can be seen as determining, or as a product of, social interaction.

CHAPTER 3

Giving and Taking Offence: Theoretical and Empirical Approaches

Abstract Following the explanation of the theoretical model of context design, this chapter reviews theoretical approaches to the study of offence. It begins by conceptualising the management of offence in terms of stance-taking. A review of the literature on online stance-taking and disagreement challenges ideas that the Internet is a broadly democratising force and shows that networked communications technologies are, like all technologies, available for exploitation in a number of ways. The focus on offence as an aspect of 'relational work' Locher and Watts (2005) draws attention to the contextual and discursive nature of impolite behaviour and suggests the appropriateness of using a context design approach to its analysis. Our discussion of this literature reveals a gap in terms of exploring how the giving and taking of offence is negotiated among 'friends' on social network sites like Facebook and its implications for changing user behaviour, the key focus of the research underpinning this book.

Keywords Echo chamber · Filter bubble · Offence · Politeness · Social norms · Stance

THE ROLE OF OFFENCE IN ONLINE RELATIONAL WORK

In *Creating Facebook*, we conceptualise the giving and taking of offence as an example of stance-taking. Stance here is a discursive construct, with people seen as performing a particular stance through linguistic and other resources. Through the act of taking a stance, people not only express their ideological beliefs but also achieve relational and identificational work (Thurlow and Jaworski 2011, p. 231); that is, people present themselves in a particular way and align (or disalign) with others through the stances they take towards a particular idea, object or person. Taking offence to something, in these terms, is a way of expressing oneself and positioning oneself in relation to others and the way they are positioning themselves.

The focus on offence as an aspect of 'relational work'—'the "work" individuals invest in negotiating relationships with others' (Locher and Watts 2005, p. 10)—draws attention to the contextual and discursive nature of impolite behaviour. Linguists adopting the traditional Brown–Levinson approach to facework and politeness (such as Herring 1994 and Vinagre 2008 in relation to online discourse) have tended to assume that utterances are inherently polite or impolite (Darics 2010). This is challenged in two main ways by the more recent model of politeness as relational work (Locher and Watts 2005). First, as aspects of relational work, 'politeness' and 'impoliteness' are re-positioned not as dichotomous orientations but as extreme ends of a spectrum of behaviour, including 'appropriate and politic' behaviour (Locher 2006, p. 255; and see Watts 1989 for use of the term 'politic'). This, as we discuss in Chap. 6, has particular relevance for a site such as Facebook which we argue is characterised by 'conviviality', that is by certain 'appropriate and politic' acts (to cite Locher 2006, p. 255) which aim to create an environment which minimises discord. Second, acts of politeness or impoliteness can only be judged as such with reference to contextual factors such as local communicative norms, speaker intentions and hearer interpretations. To put this in terms of stance, acts of stance-taking serve to dynamically construct the object of the stance (Thurlow and Jaworski 2011). This is recognised in studies looking at aggression online; for example, it is often people's responses to a particular behaviour that lead to it being understood as aggressive or antagonistic (Angouri and Tseliga 2010; Hardaker 2010). As a result, what is considered aggressive, impolite or offensive will vary between communities or online sites and will change over time. This contextual approach to online aggression is particularly relevant to our exploration of what acts of offence reveal about processes of context design—that is what different stances towards an act of communication on Facebook can tell us about the dynamic co-construction and negotiation of site norms and practices. While Locher (2006, p. 264) suggests that we need to determine the 'norms of appropriateness' against which judgements about polite/impolite behaviour can be made, we turn this around to explore what *acts of offence* (in which people cause and take offence) can tell us about people's differing perceptions of appropriate behaviour. Indeed, we explore whether acts of offence can, in fact, serve to trigger the discursive construction of interactive norms and social boundaries (see Tiidenberg 2015 on the discursive function of conflicts around re-posted erotic selfies).

With reference to social media (and specifically online advice sites), Locher (2006) points out that, although shared evaluations are likely to arise in repeated interactions over time, users unfamiliar with a site may bring norms of appropriateness that diverge from those which dominate there. What Locher (2006) does not consider is how the co-construction of impolite acts would unfold in semi-public, shifting spaces such as Facebook, where people who do not have regular sustained interactions can come into fleeting contact. The question we seek to address through the *Creating Facebook* project is, therefore, how participants respond to a behaviour they find offensive in contexts, where shared norms of appropriateness (or common social/political views) cannot necessarily be assumed because of the complex way in which audiences are configured and because of the unpredictable trajectories of people's posts—two factors which are intrinsic to the communicative experience on a site like Facebook.

Conflict and Lack of Engagement Online

The history of research into online communication suggests that social media can act as a convenient and powerful means by which people from diverse backgrounds but with shared orientations, values and goals can come together, but that the Internet does not always foster debate and engagement between people with different views and beliefs, as was touted by early promoters of the capabilities of online communication. Instead, conflict often emerges in response to people's adoption of adversarial stances to others' views, encouraged by Internet affordances and shaped by immediate social norms. It is against this backdrop that the significance of offending on Facebook can be understood as emerging from the particular communicative dynamics afforded by the site and the way people use it.

With the advent of the Internet and its emergence as a mainstream cultural tool, there was a short period of excitement about its potential for ensuring equality and democracy by promoting public participation on the part of typically under-represented groups, such as women (Graddol and Swann 1989). Although this view was quickly challenged by studies exploring discrimination and aggression online (e.g. Herring et al. 1995), vestiges of this early optimism continue to be found in descriptions of the potential of social media for breaking down barriers and bringing people together into online 'affinity spaces' characterised by shared goals and emergent norms (Gee 2005), as well as in a host of studies identifying and detailing online affiliation and community (Drasovean and Tagg 2015; Zappavigna 2014). However, the nature of communication in an online space depends on how the particular affordances of a site are exploited by its users and the social practices and norms that develop within local communities. As such, Internet affordances such as the possibility of anonymity, the physical distance between interlocutors and a relative lack of social cues may enhance democratic participation, but they may just as well encourage repressive and confrontational behaviour (MacKinnon 2011). A growing body of literature focused on acts of *flaming*—'displaying hostility by insulting, swearing or using otherwise offensive language' (Moor et al. 2010, p. 1537)—also highlights an important distinction between users who *intend* to offend and provoke conflict (often those engaged in cyberbullying or trolling), and users who offend through disagreeing with others, putting forward their own views or inadvertently flouting the norms and expectations of others (the focus of our study).

Hostile and polarised debate has been particularly associated with the media-sharing site YouTube, both among commenters (Bou-Franch and Garcés-Conejos Blitvich 2014; Lorenzo-Dus et al. 2011; Moor et al. 2010; van Zoonen et al. 2011) and video posters (Lange 2014; Pihlaja 2011, 2014). This tendency for polarised debate has been put down to a process of *deindividuation* (initially proposed by Reicher et al. 1995) associated both with groups and with anonymous, disembodied online contexts, in which people lose their sense of individual identity and instead take on the beliefs and aims of the group as a whole (see, for example Bou-Franch and Garcés-Conejos Blitvich 2014; Moor et al. 2010). Processes of deindividuation can encourage people to adhere more strongly to immediate group norms than they would in other contexts, to oppose in a more extreme fashion the norms of 'the

Other' (Lee 2007) and to define themselves in 'classic us versus them terms' (Lorenzo-Dus et al. 2011, p. 2591). These ideological expressions of group identity can lead to an unintended escalation of aggression (Moor et al. 2010). In the potentially polarised environment of a YouTube comment thread, what seems to trigger conflict is not so much that people post offensive views or even the fact that people are offended by others' views, but the often aggressive and provocative way in which people are likely to respond to a perceived offence (Bou-Franch and Garcés-Conejos Blitvich 2014). In other words, conflict is caused by people taking an overtly hostile stance to an online action, dynamically re-construing the original action as offensive and encouraging equally confrontational positionings by others.

Despite the aggressively hostile environment on YouTube, it appears that users in general are often not aiming to provoke, but are instead intent on expressing disagreement and putting forward a particular viewpoint. For example, in Moor et al. (2010) survey of users who had been involved in acts of apparent flaming, most reported that the purpose of their comment was to state an opposing opinion, with a number justifying their aggressive comments with reference to the poor quality of the video they were criticising and others suggesting that they were responding to an offensive act. Despite these motivations, online confrontation of the sort seen to take place on YouTube does not, for the most part, appear to involve productive engagement with others' views (Chun and Walters 2011; Hirzalla et al. 2013; van Zoonen et al. 2011). Pihlaja (2011) gives a vivid illustration of the way the site can bring together groups with strong opposing moral views—in this case, Christians and atheists—but not necessarily in a way likely to lead to mutual understanding. In one video interaction—an exchange formed of a series of home-produced talking head videos—an atheist user starts a debate on the development of stem cell research, which he sees as being delayed by Christian objections, but the exchange rapidly deteriorates into a series of personal insults based around criticisms of the users' respective behaviour on the site, with the atheist eventually denouncing the Christian user as a self-styled 'Pope of YouTube'. Here, the histrionic behaviour, stylised videos and public platform suggest that the aggressive behaviour is a performance designed to appeal to and unite like-minded others (as also suggested by the comments on the videos), rather than an act of engagement with the 'Other'. Similarly, in their study of polarisation in comments to a video on youth homosexuality, Bou-Franch and

Garcés-Conejos Blitvich (2014) found that participants tended to leave one comment and withdraw, and that conflicts were rarely resolved, suggesting that people are not interested in engaging in extended debate or in having their views changed. Chun and Walters (2011) point to the nature of the technology itself in explaining this tendency for users not to engage more deeply, suggesting that sites like YouTube 'may encourage simplistic readings of social others … limited by the website's architectural constraints' (p. 256); comments, for example are constrained in length in a way that encourages people to be pithy and to rely on readily available tropes.

A number of studies suggest that, by using computer technology to seek out like-minded others, people are not so much broadening their worldviews but reinforcing existing ones (Gee and Hayes 2011; Sunstein 2002). Selective information exposure of this sort on the Internet risks creating an 'echo chamber' or 'filter bubble' in which people hear only those views with which they already agree (Garrett 2009a, b; Iyengar and Hahn 2009; Kosinski et al. 2013)—a process we referred to earlier as 'ghetto-ization' (Jones and Hafner 2012: 126) and which risks further polarising debate (Conover et al. 2011). For example, in their analysis of comments on TED.com videos on the subject of food, Drasovean and Tagg (2015) found that commenters adhered to shared ideologies relating to organic and junk food, and that these shared worldviews formed the basis for discursively constructed affiliations on the site. Elsewhere, echo chambers have been found to be particularly likely to shape political discussions. In their study of 3.8 million US tweets and retweets, for example, Barbera et al. (2015) found highly polarised debate likely in discussion of party politics around the 2012 presidential election and the 2014 State of the Union address, with controversial issues such as a school shooting initially generating cross-ideological discussion of the tragedy and then becoming increasingly polarised as participants started discussing gun control policy. Discussion of less politically sensitive issues exhibited greater ideological diversity. The tendency for social media to create such silos is recognised beyond academia, as evidenced, for example by *The Guardian*'s discussion of the impact of Facebook's 'confirmation bias' during the 2016 US presidential contest between Hillary Clinton and Donald Trump (Bixby 2016).

As suggested in the literature reviewed above, online conflict is often seen as being shaped by the affordances of digital technology, and by the particular functionalities of sites such as YouTube, which might be seen to encourage extreme behaviour by allowing for anonymous, multiparty interactions through comments. Equally important in shaping the communicative dynamic, however, are the social norms that develop within localised communities, as well as the perceived audience and communicative purposes. Local social norms are important not only in determining what counts as offensive in any one context—for example Lange (2014) finds that ranting about YouTube can be considered appropriate by users who sympathise with the ranters' complaints; and Page (2014a) finds that 'fraping' (hacking into someone's Facebook account and posting from it) can, in certain situations, be considered an act of solidarity—but also in shaping the wider communicative dynamics that create opportunities for conflict. Pihlaja (2016), for example compares the comments made in response to adult videos posted on the popular online video provider, Pornhub (a pornographic video sharing website), with those made on other sites like YouTube. Despite similarities between the format and affordances of Pornhub and YouTube, he found little evidence of interaction in the former and, in particular, almost no sign of antagonism between commenters. He puts this down to the specific nature of interacting with pornographic videos, which encourage a viewer to express and describe their own pleasure and fantasies, as well as the development of local, site-specific social norms. These shared norms include the acceptability of comments expressing sexual desire which involve what might be considered obscene language on YouTube, and which make antagonistic interaction less likely. In short, viewing on Pornhub is experienced as a solitary, rather than a community, act and is thus less likely to lead to conflict than on YouTube.

On Twitter, disagreements can be high profile. Take as examples, the tweets traded in 2016 between the US presidential nominees Hillary Clinton and Donald Trump (see Zillman 2016) or the disagreement (later acknowledged as a misunderstanding) in mid-2015 between pop stars Taylor Swift and Nicki Minaj (*The Guardian* 2015). However, research into interactions between groups where disagreement would be expected (i.e. on the opposite sides of the Israel-Palestine, US Democrat-Republican and FC Barcelona-Real Madrid divides) by Liu and Weber (2014) suggests that users are more inclined to interact with like-minded users, or what they term 'ideological-friends', than those with whom they would be expected to disagree (p. 341). Moreover, when there are interactions across the assumed ideological divides, they found that those interactions tended to be rational rather than abusive, suggesting that Twitter may foster agreement rather than the conflict that the more high-profile cases might suggest.

The propensity for conflict to happen on Twitter is also likely linked to how the site is used and how different people use it. Liu and Weber (2014) point to differences in how users of different status engage in discussions: those with fewer followers are more likely to initiate challenges to those in 'authority' (those in the top 1% in terms of followers), but are in turn more likely to be ignored. While not explicitly mentioned by the researchers, the willingness for lower status users to directly challenge high-profile figures may reflect the non-reciprocal participation structure of Twitter (i.e. the fact that it is possible to 'follow' any public account on the site, but without the guarantee that the other user will return the gesture), suggesting that affordances of the site play some role in the potential for Twitter to act as a space for dispute and conflict. In addition, instances of aggression on Twitter may also point to the heterogeneous discourse structure of the site (Page 2014a, p. 199); that is, the fact that the platform is used by different people in different ways.

Despite the growing literature on online conflict, there is relatively little research into the taking and giving of offence within the semi-public context of an individual's Facebook newsfeed. What research there is, however, suggests a general avoidance of conflict in exchanges on the site, in marked contrast to the type of behaviour observed on YouTube and (in some cases) on Twitter. While public Facebook profiles can be used for similar ends as YouTube (see Pihlaja's [forthcoming] discussion of the YouTube evangelist Joshua Feuerstein's use of a public Facebook account to publicise his videos), the communicative dynamics are likely to differ where the profile is used as a personal page rather than to put forward a public position or agenda. In personal Facebook accounts, the privacy settings tend to limit access to a user's Friends and thus the audience generally comprises people the user knows from various times and places in their lives. At the same time, the personal connections established through Facebook tend to constitute 'weak ties' (Granovetter 1973)—the people with whom we have more tenuous connections such as friends of friends or acquaintances—and are therefore more fragile; that is, subject to hiding or defriending in problematic discussions (Grevet et al. 2014; John and Dvir-Gvirsman 2015; Rainnie and Smith 2012). On the other hand, strong ties—the people we have close relationships with—are more likely to provoke a confrontation (McLaughlin and Vitak 2012, p. 310).

The apparent goal for Facebook users, therefore, is to use strategies to keep the peace (Lang and Barton 2015; Rainnie and Smith 2012). Our own *Creating Facebook* project suggests that people's various offline social roles and responsibilities—as parent, employee, family member—often remain relevant on a site like Facebook and serve to constrain or influence people's behaviour as they take care to monitor and curate the way they present themselves (see Tagg and Seargeant 2017). In other studies, people have been described as showing reluctance to post on Facebook issues that might offend or be divisive (Sveningson 2014; Rainnie and Smith 2012 and see Takahashi 2010 for a similar observation about the social network site Mixi in Japan), with Sleeper et al. (2013) noting that people would be more inclined to share opinions and ideas if they could be targeted better at specific sets of people. In other words, as shown in the Chap. 4, the intradiverse nature of people's Facebook friends means that people have to do a great deal of maintenance work and/or avoid posting.

Summary: Conflict and Context Design

In summary, then, the *Creating Facebook* project conceptualises offence-taking as a stance which is discursively performed within a particular space and according to local expectations and practices. As such, instances where people are offended not only reveals their underlying values and media ideologies but also points to the negotiation and ongoing co-construction of contextually relevant norms. Our conceptualisation of offence as a discursive construct has two main implications for understanding context design as a significant communicative dynamic on sites like Facebook. First, examples where people's communicative expectations have not been met can serve as a heuristic for exploring what these communicative expectations are and how they might shape people's behaviour online. This rests on the assumption that people may become particularly aware of their own values in instances where these are challenged or disrupted. Second, the actions that people take in response to being offended provide an illustration of context design 'in action', as people shape their future behaviour according to their ideas about present or past misdemeanours on the site. Given the particular affordances of Facebook, it appears that users may be less likely to respond aggressively or confrontationally to a perceived act of offence, and instead act more covertly to avoid or mitigate offence. This has particular implications for processes of context design, and how these processes shape communication on Facebook.

CHAPTER 4

Social Media and Intradiverse Networks

Abstract This chapter draws on our sample of Facebook users to explore how networks facilitated by this particular social media platform give rise to acts of offence, and shape people's responses to being offended or giving offence. As was touched upon in the previous chapter, there has been increasing recognition of differences between online platforms or modes of communication and a growing focus on how particular communities exploit or deal with the affordances of online technology in distinct ways for their own purposes. Facebook, although often grouped together with sites like Twitter, YouTube and Reddit in the broader category of 'social media', represents a particular type of online site and thus exhibits a distinct communicative dynamic (Androutsopoulos 2005). In order to explain this we introduce the concept of *intradiversity*—the way in which the audience that people are writing for on Facebook is shaped by complexes of personal networks, individual experiences and mutual friendships, rather than being organised along traditionally defined community lines. This is illustrated though an explanation of the network which provides the sample for our research study.

Keywords Intradiversity · Ego-centred · Online network Research participants

Facebook as an Ego-Centred Social Media Context

In this chapter, we introduce our notion of intradiversity as a way of understanding the particular type of network that communication on Facebook—and its particular configuration of affordances—gives rise to. While early linguistic studies of the internet tended to treat digitally mediated communication as a homogenous issue—going so far, in some cases, as to suggest it could be viewed as a distinct language variety (Crystal 2006)—there has a been increasing recognition of differences between online platforms or modes of communication and a growing focus on how particular individuals and groups exploit or deal with the affordances of online technology in distinct ways for their own purposes. Facebook, although often grouped together with sites like Twitter, YouTube and Reddit in the broader category of social media, represents a particular type of online site and thus exhibits a distinct communicative dynamic (Androutsopoulos 2015; Tagg and Seargeant 2016).

As a communicative space, Facebook is shaped to some extent by its underlying architecture and by the purposes for which users are encouraged to use it (see Chap. 1). Although some profile details can be seen by all users and settings can allow for general public access, Facebook is not by default a public site, but instead it is often described as semi-public. Networks and audiences on Facebook are *ego-centred* in the sense that entry can to some extent be controlled by the profile owners and is often limited to people with whom a profile owner has a pre-existing relationship. In Baym's (2010, p. 90) terms, Facebook tends to encourage a kind of 'networked individualism', 'in which each person sits at the centre of his or her own personal community'. A user can decide who to add to their list of Friends and in this way determine, to a degree, who has access to their posts. It is partly as a result of this process of audience building that Facebook and similar media have been defined in terms of context collapse, and that research has focused on the complex of issues we examined in Chap. 2. As was discussed earlier, the fact that each Friend has their own interconnected ego-centred network leads to potential 'leakage', in that posts to which a friend has commented may appear in their Friends' newsfeeds so that one's posts can become visible to Friends of Friends, leading to a somewhat unpredictable text trajectory.

The impact of this participation structure, we argue, is threefold. The first implication is that users are not by default performing in front of strangers or the public at large, as they may consider themselves to be when posting on Twitter or making a YouTube video. Instead, they are performing predominantly in front of people they know, albeit that they may not, at any one time, be quite sure which part of their potential audience is viewing their contributions. As discussed in Chap. 2, it is likely that there will be some impact on a poster's style from 'overhearers' (the potential audience for a post), in that it appears that people are more constrained in how/what they post from consideration of the people at the periphery of their friends list (acquaintances, distant family members) than strangers happening on their posts or what their close friends may think of them (Tagg 2013, and see Chap. 1). Users appear to respond to this situation in different ways: it can prompt them to produce bland posts designed not to offend (as we shall be exploring in greater detail with the data from the current study); it can encourage them to actively address certain others by enacting group identity; and it can lead to a range of audience design strategies (Tagg and Seargeant 2014).

The second implication is that the ego-centred nature of Facebook networks may impact on the apparent tendency for many users to focus on self-presentation as a goal in its own right. In particular, it appears from the wider literature that Facebook may encourage people to present themselves, by means of what they post and the connections they make, in a consistently good light as if every day were what Baron (2007) calls 'my best day'. Studies suggest there are norms against introducing negative topics on Facebook, or posting unflattering photos, and that users are often very aware that information and pictures posted online offer a 'skewed' self-presentation (McLaughlin and Vitak 2011, p. 306). We hypothesise that this focus on self-presentation—where it happens—may suggest a situation in which stance-taking occurs as part of a wider identity project and where users may be particularly unlikely to put forward an unpopular or contradictory view. As we shall see in the next chapter, our research as a part of *Creating Facebook* suggests that these and other factors tend, in the case of Facebook, to lead to a situation which encourages conviviality across the network, rather than flaming and other aggressive behaviour.

Intradiversity

Finally, we argue that the third implication of the participation structure is that the audience, which a status update constructs is *intradiverse* in the sense that it is shaped by complexes of personal networks, individual experiences and mutual friendships, rather than being organised along traditionally defined community lines. Our argument sits in opposition to other scholarly accounts of the internet, which tends to be discussed in the research literature as fostering contexts not of intradiversity but of superdiversity (Androutsopoulos and Juffermans 2014). The concept of superdiversity emerged as a way of understanding the increasingly complex and layered waves of migration characterising British cities from the 1990s onwards, which, it was argued, called for a need for social policy to abandon the assumption that migrants belong to fixed, homogenous communities (Vertovec 2007). Seen as a lens through which to understand social relations, superdiversity encourages us to challenge the assumption that straightforward connections can be made between individuals and larger social categories (such as ethnicity, gender or language-background). The internet has often been described in the literature as fostering superdiversity either by enabling migrants to maintain overseas contacts or by bringing together people from different cultural backgrounds into one online space, often around a shared interest such as football (Kytölä, forthcoming) or hiphop (Varis and Wang 2011).

On sites such as Facebook, however, the audience that a person interacts with is unlikely, for the most part, to be superdiverse because, as we have seen, the site is bounded and centred round one person's connections. Instead, we describe such communities as intradiverse in the sense that the audience for any Facebook post is likely not unpredictably superdiverse (and nor is it likely shaped primarily by social characteristics such as ethnicity or national identity or by a shared interest) but instead exhibits a diversity shaped (and limited) by the profile owner's life trajectory. The links within the network which comprise this possible audience are built up from encounters across the individual's biography, and while diversity is often present (in the way, for example, a person will have relatives from their hometown, friends from their college years, acquaintances they met on their travels and so on), all the links will share some initial affinity with the individual which produced the link in the first place. At the same time, however, intradiversity heightens the potential for coming into contact with views or practices which differ from one's own (the college friend will be sharing the same communicative space as the travel acquaintance) and it thus raises the likelihood of people being offended and of inadvertently causing offence. In order to give a more vivid explanation of how this dynamic works in practice, we present, in the next section, the network used for gathering the data for this study, and look at the ways in which it can be said to be intradiverse.

Make-up of the Network

As explained in Chap. 1, the research centred on the Facebook network of one of the authors of the book. This was a deliberate methodological decision, designed to generate a particular sample of respondents (as explained below). This author first joined Facebook in early 2005. At that time Facebook was only open to people associated with certain universities and other institutions in North America and the UK. However, as Facebook opened up and began to be used by a wider audience the researcher gained contacts from other areas of her life, such as her family, old school friends and co-workers. After graduating, she lived in Japan and China for a number of years, where she taught English and undertook postgraduate study, meaning that her network expanded to include her colleagues (mostly teachers), new friends, pupils and fellow students. She then moved back to the UK to take up doctoral study, which increased the number of research students and academic-related contacts in her network. In addition to the friends who can be directly related to those key stages, she also gained connections whilst travelling, through friends and so on. It is worth noting that the researcher has met or had some form of online contact with all of the members of her Facebook network; in other words, she is not 'Friends' with anybody who could be termed a 'stranger' [Hampton et al. (2011) suggest that most adult Facebook users have few Friends whom they have never met in person, noting that Facebook and other social networks are increasingly used to maintain close social ties]. This is in contrast to the variety (or lack thereof) of contacts she has on other social platforms; for example on Twitter she follows and is followed by a number of people she has had no online or offline contact with, but on WhatsApp she interacts only with people she has a reasonably close offline relationship with.

In order to provide a visualisation of this network, the researcher looked through her Friends list and mapped the main stages of her personal trajectory in which she became acquainted with each Friend in her network. These different life stages are depicted in Fig. 4.1, where the size of the group represents the number of Friends the researcher had from that group at the time of the project (the total number of her Friends at that time was 384). As with any network connected to

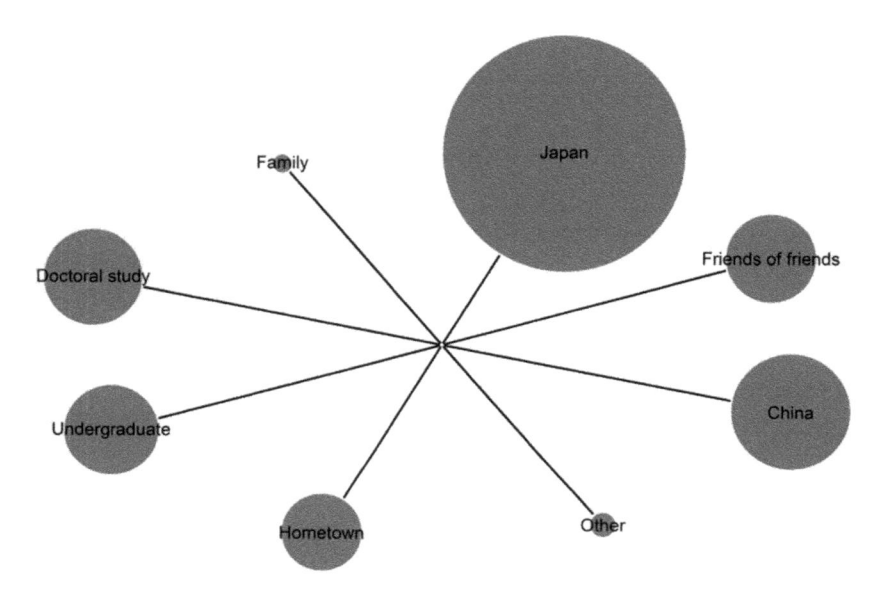

Fig. 4.1 Make-up of the researcher's Facebook network based on the different stages of her life trajectory

an individual, the one used as the basis for this study is highly unlikely to be representative of the general population of Facebook users, and even within the network, Friends the researcher met in some places (e.g. Japan) or Friends with certain associations or interests (e.g. language learning and teaching) are more common than Friends in other groups (e.g. family). However, the different places and ways in which the researcher gained contacts produces a pattern of intradiversity, as the concept has been described above.

In all, 141 responses were subject to analysis. Residents of 26 different countries responded to the questionnaire, as demonstrated in Fig. 4.2. Most respondents reported to reside in the UK ($n = 50$, 35%), South Korea ($n = 24$, 17%), or the USA ($n = 19$, 14%). The number of participants in the UK reflects the researcher's home base and location at the time of the research. The number of respondents in South Korea and the USA reflects the number of close friends she made mostly while teaching English in Asia.

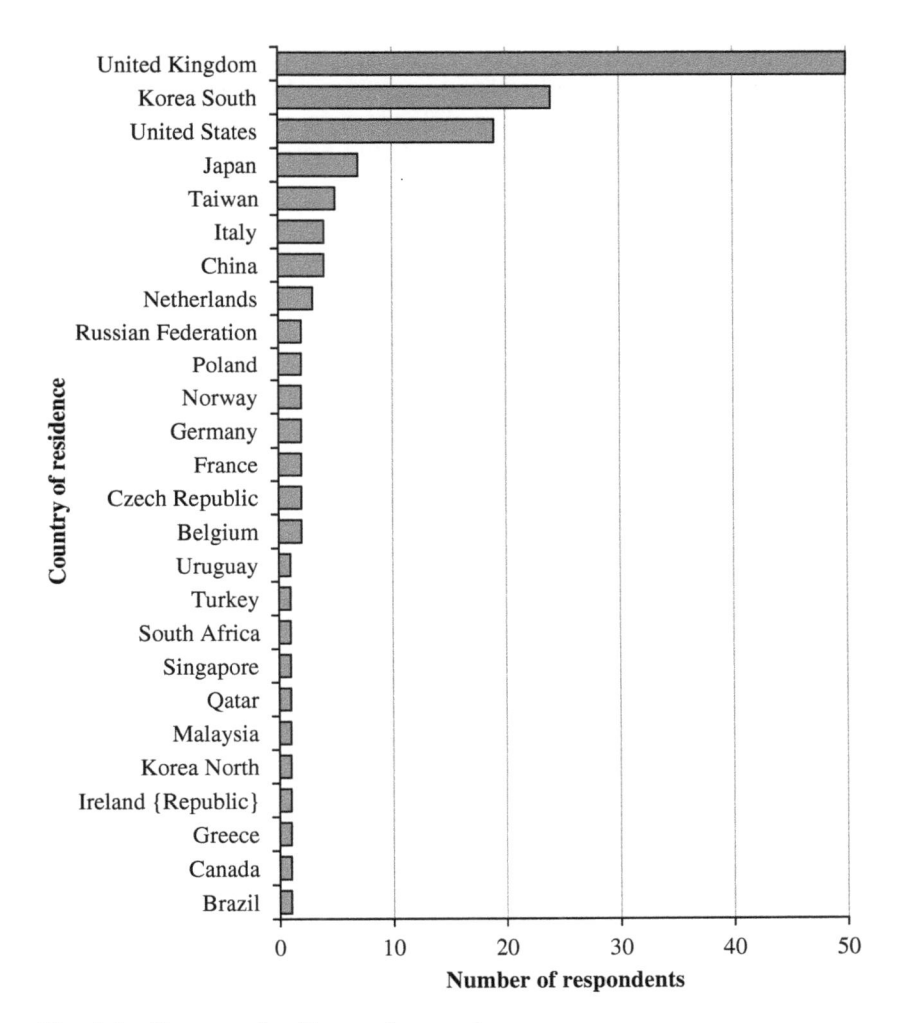

Fig. 4.2 Country of residence of respondents

Respondents were asked to explain the language(s) they use on Facebook. Given that the questionnaire was only offered in English, it should be of little surprise that almost all respondents ($n = 138$, 98%) said they used English on Facebook. Some respondents claimed to only be able to use English (e.g. 'I can't speak anything else'). However, in addition to English, 25 other languages were also mentioned. These other languages are shown in Fig. 4.3, the next most commonly mentioned languages being Japanese ($n = 22$) and Korean ($n = 19$).

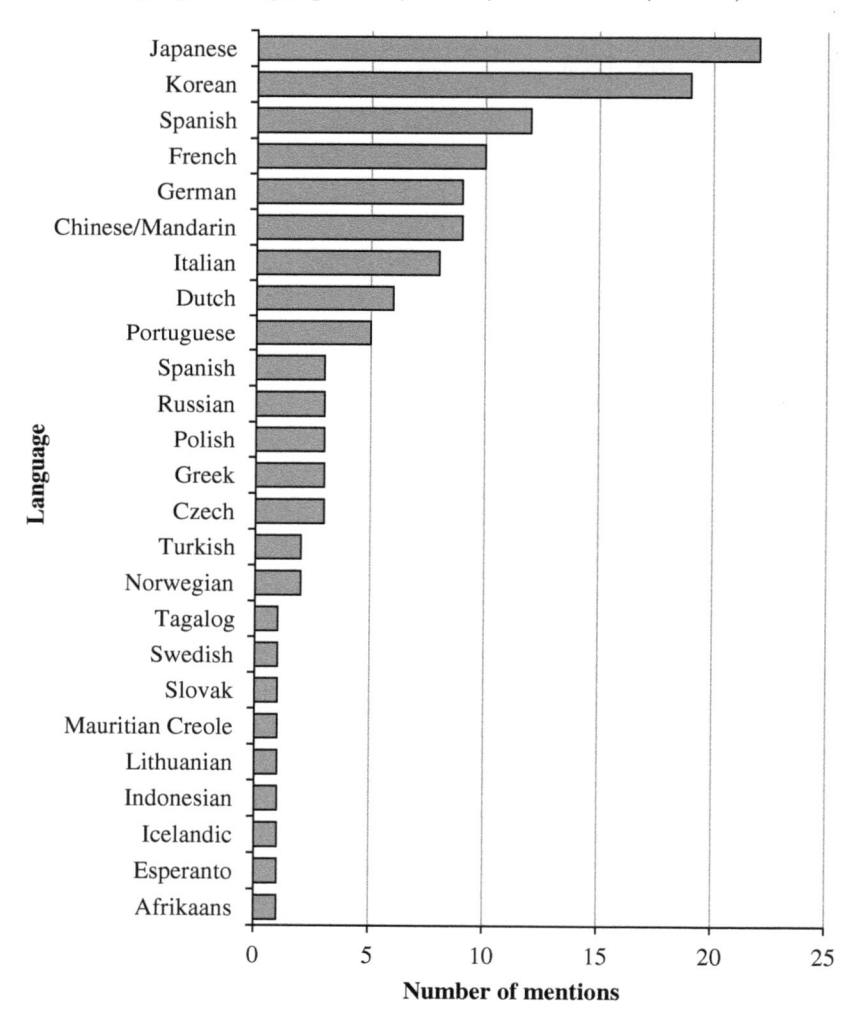

Fig. 4.3 Languages other than English that respondents reported using on Facebook

The survey was completed by more female respondents ($n = 89$, 63%) than male ($n = 52$, 37%). In terms of age (see Fig. 4.4), most respondents ($n = 129$, 89%) defined themselves as being in the two groups closest to the age of the researcher: 22–30 or 31–45 ($n = 57$, 40%, and $n = 69$, 49% respectively). Most other respondents classified themselves into the 45–60 group ($n = 12$, 9%). The relative lack of younger respondents ($n = 3$, 2%) and the complete lack of responses from anyone in the Over 60 group is likely to be a simple reflection of the age range of the network, but it is also worth noting that one person who would fall into the Over 60 group said to the researcher that she did not complete the questionnaire because she only used Facebook to see what others were doing and never to post, making much of the questionnaire irrelevant. If other older users also behave in this way, it could explain why there were no responses from that group.

Respondents were asked to provide an estimation of the number of their Facebook Friends and how many of those Friends they commonly interact with (see Figs. 4.5 and 4.6). Some reported fewer but the majority ($n = 80$, 57%) reported to have in excess of 300 Friends. The number of Friends that respondents reported interacting with, however, was fewer: around 70% ($n = 101$) report to commonly interact with 50 Friends or fewer, and only 13 (9%) claim to interact with more than 100.

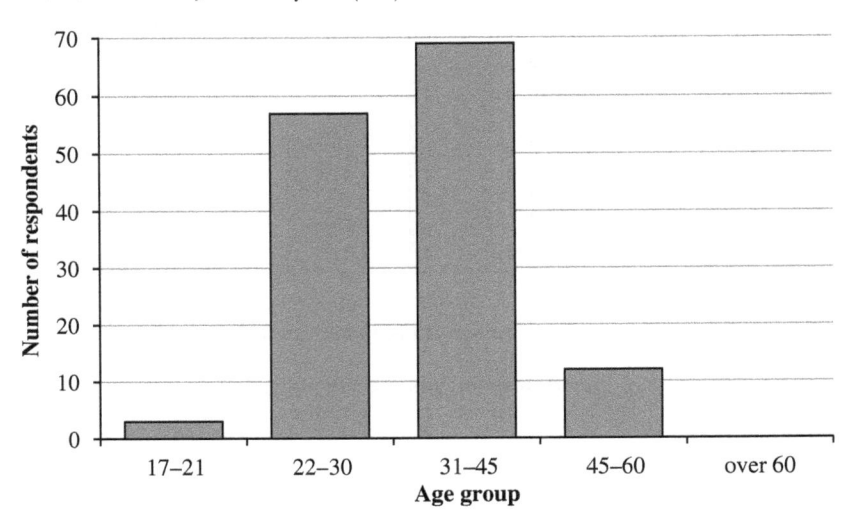

Fig. 4.4 Age of respondents

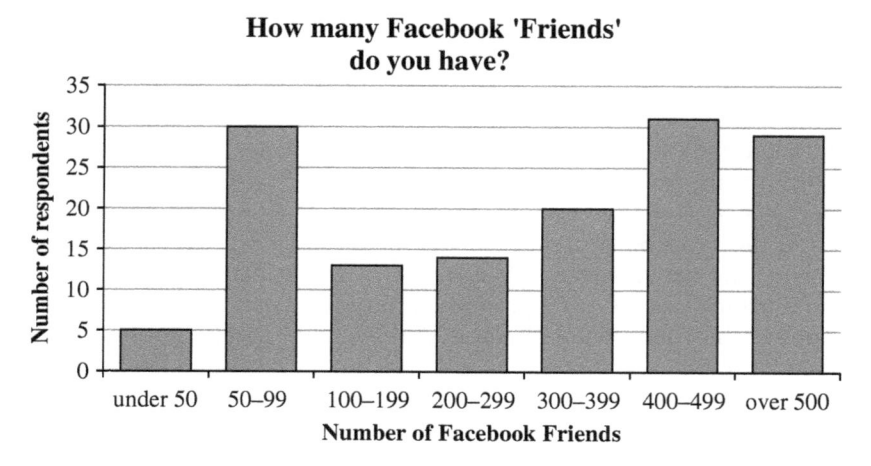

Fig. 4.5 Number of Facebook Friends respondents have

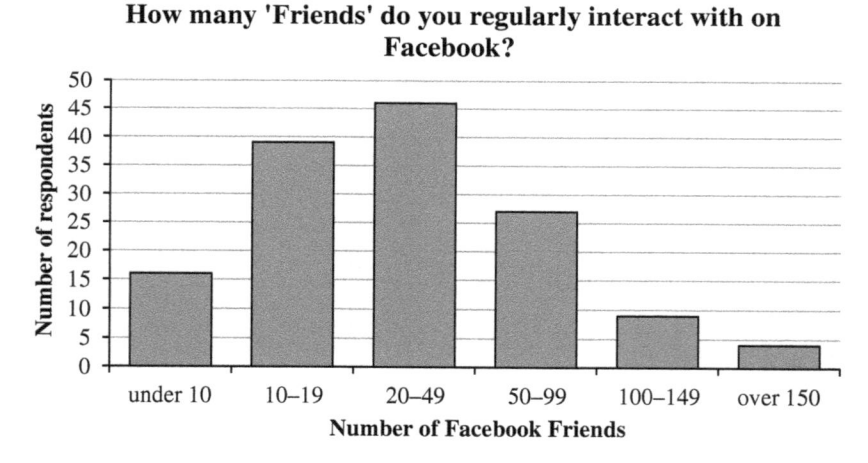

Fig. 4.6 Number of Friends respondents regularly interact with on Facebook

In terms of Facebook usage (see Figs. 4.7, 4.8 and 4.9), the respondents mostly reported going onto the site throughout the day ($n = 104$, 74%) or once a day ($n = 25$, 18%), with far fewer reporting to use it just

How often do you go onto Facebook?

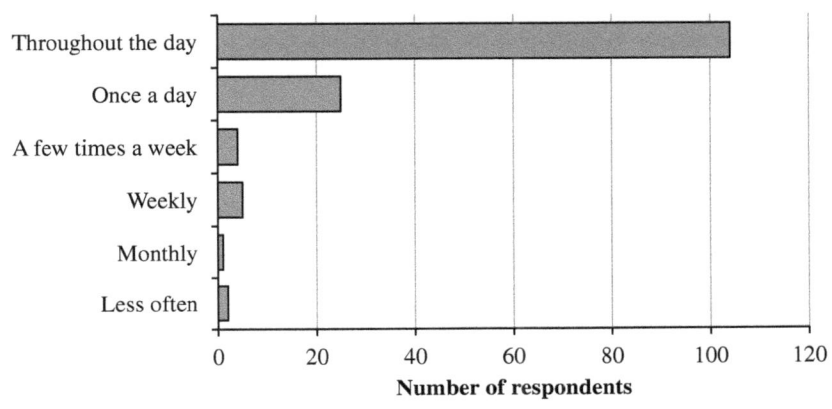

Fig. 4.7 How often respondents go onto Facebook

a few times per week or less ($n = 12$, 6%). However, there was a broader spread in the reported frequency of posting to Facebook: while a number of respondents also reported to post throughout the day ($n = 26$, 18%), most reported to post a few times per week ($n = 38$, 27%) or weekly ($n = 29$, 28%). In terms of the reasons respondents reported to use Facebook, some reported to use it mainly for messaging people ($n = 15$, 11%), posting status updates or photos ($n = 6$, 4% and $n = 4$, 3%, respectively), or other uses ($n = 11$, 8%, often keeping up with people), but the vast majority reported to use it for looking at their news feeds ($n = 104$, 74%).

Finally, as noted, three participants were then interviewed. They have been given the pseudonyms Heather, Jacob, and Jessica. Heather is a friend and former colleague of the researcher, who is in the 22–30 age group. She used to live in Japan, but now resides in the UK. Jacob is a friend of a friend, is from the USA and now lives and works in South Korea. He is also in the 22–30 age group. Jessica is again a friend of a friend, is from Canada but also lives and works in South Korea. She is in the 31–45 age group. Note that quotations taken from their interviews throughout this chapter are referred to by their pseudonyms, as given above.

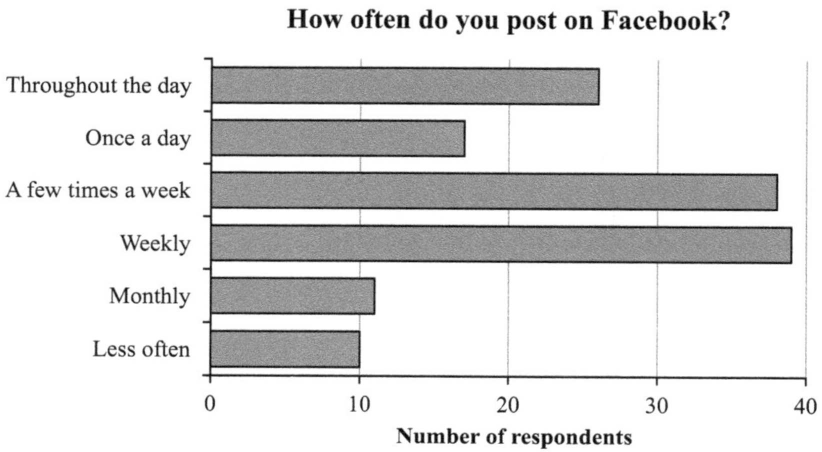
How often do you post on Facebook?
Throughout the day
Once a day
A few times a week
Weekly
Monthly
Less often
0
10
20
30
40
Number of respondents

Fig. 4.8 How often respondents post on Facebook

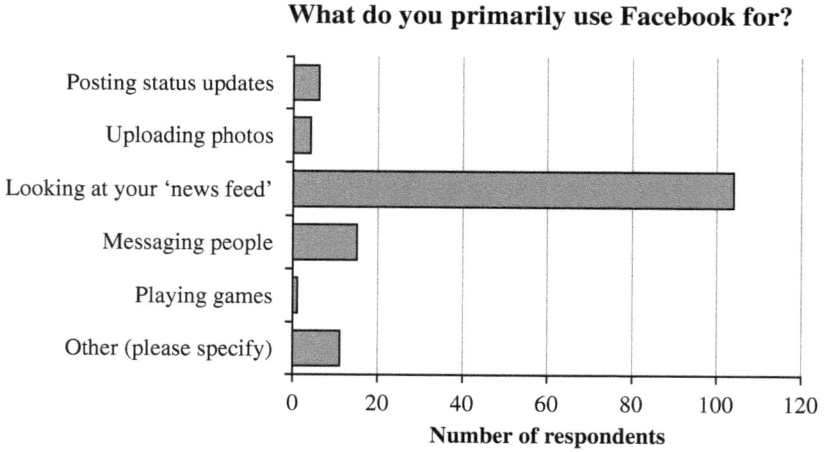
What do you primarily use Facebook for?
Posting status updates
Uploading photos
Looking at your 'news feed'
Messaging people
Playing games
Other (please specify)
0
20
40
60
80
100
120
Number of respondents

Fig. 4.9 Respondents' primary uses of Facebook

From the above description, we can begin to piece together what makes this network—like other Facebook networks—intradiverse, at least In the sense of explicit social categories such as geographical location and geographical background, culture, language, gender and age. The network does not map onto a homogenous community in terms of these categorisations: the participants are located in 26 different countries, they speak 26 languages between them and include a range of ages. At the same time there are observable patterns in this composition, which relate (as we have seen) to the node user's life trajectory. Despite the apparent diversity of the network, most participants do or have resided in one of the three countries in which the researcher has lived, and speak the three languages most closely associated with each; and most users fall into a particular age category. In other words, the way in which the network was constructed as a result of the researcher's travels and life stages operates as a constraint on its diversity. Rather than being constrained by shared geographical background, for example the diversity is constrained by the mutual relationships of the participants to the researcher.

Looking Beyond Explicit Social Categories in Intradiversity

Elements that contribute to the intradiverse nature of the network come from a number of different levels. Alongside the explicit social categories discussed above, there are somewhat less tangible social categories like class and education. Although not captured directly in our survey, we speculate that these are also relevant to understanding the precise diversity of the network. One possible implication of these variables is indicated in the description of her own network provided by one of our interviewees, Heather. Heather claims that her network is diverse in terms of where her Friends are in the world but not necessarily in terms of 'class'. She notes that most of her Friends are university-educated and have travelled, and that some are also united by their mutual interest in amateur dramatics.

(3) It is diverse in that they are all from different people, different places sorry, but at same time I would say that … there is a certain kind of class in there I guess. The kind of people that are interested in … theatre and the arts, generally speaking, they are not coming from a working class background I guess. … So the people who I have on my Facebook are the people who I know what to post and what not to. [Heather, interview]

As this quotation suggests, there are likely to be a number of other implicit areas of diversity which shape online behaviour in idiosyncratic ways. These discursive or submerged variables include values or patterns of shared value systems; personal experiences; and personal expectations and aspirations, as well as variables related to Facebook itself, such as expectations around Facebook use. Finally, it is worth noting that, unlike other online communities, this network as a whole does not affiliate around a particular topic, activity or interest, other than a shared use of Facebook. The only thing that all participants are likely to have—and what brings them together in this shared space—is their mutual relationship with the researcher.

These discursive or submerged variables are ones we need to look at the qualitative data itself for, in order to build a picture of their influence. Indeed, as will be seen, the diversity that leads to acts of offence seems to be most strongly related to the expression of people's values, which are themselves shaped by personal experiences and aspirations. More explicit social categories are not as relevant, because despite the diversity in these Facebook networks, people affiliate primarily around shared values and outlook, and their management of their Facebook is driven by these more implicit variables (i.e. they may exclude or unfriend people who do not seem to share their views or expectations). In the next section, we move on to explore what the responses given by survey participants and interviewees reveal about the intradiversity of their own online networks, as highlighted in particular by instances of miscommunication.

CHAPTER 5

The Impact of Intradiversity on Online Offence

Abstract This chapter continues the focus on intradiversity by exploring how our data sheds light on people's awareness of the intradiverse nature of their online audience on Facebook and how this awareness shapes their online behaviour. It does this through detailed analysis of the strategies that people report using in order to manage their online interactions, the reasons for why offence is given or taken, and the actions people take towards it within the context of constructing and maintaining their online communities. This analysis builds on our discussion in Chap. 4 around the structuring of diversity on Facebook with reference to explicit social categories (e.g. age), by highlighting other more submerged sources of difference, including education, personal values and political beliefs, as well as the particular kind of relationship that the node user has with each of their Facebook Friends. As we shall see, people's awareness of the variety of worldviews that make up the potential audience for their online communication shape their decisions regarding what to post in various ways.

Keywords Awareness · Dis(Identification) · Friends · Intradiversity Politics · Privacy

User Awareness of Intradiversity

In this chapter, we analyse data in order to flesh out our concept of intradiversity. How does the data from the study show the ways in which people are aware of and respond to the intradiverse context in which their communication takes place (and which they then construct as a frame for the way this communication is styled and how they imagine it will be interpreted)? In order to outline the perception of intradiversity in the network, we focus on the ways that concerns over the giving and taking of offence—and concerns over what is seen as offensive behaviour—provide a touchstone for the way people perceive Facebook as a space for communication. A majority of people in the survey (60%) reported that they had, at some stage, taken offence to something posted on Facebook, and this issue thus provides an insightful way of looking at more general ideas about communication on the site. As will be shown, in terms of people's responses to attitudes to offence, what we call intradiversity is seen by respondents as a key contributing factor, and thus in examining what causes offence and why we are able to draw out a clearer empirical picture of the nature and consequences of the intradiverse networks that exist on Facebook.

The first point to make is that many of our study participants were very conscious of the intradiversity in their network. This was particularly evident in the interviews (as illustrated earlier in relation to Heather's network) probably because of the extended opportunity the interviewees had for elaborating on their responses. Their statements allude to the complex ways in which intradiversity can be perceived on the site. For example, Jessica—who is part of a network of US wives of Korean men—makes distinctions in her Friends' network between the different experiences of women married to Korean men who are based in the US, those who have just arrived with their husbands in Korea, and those who have been living in Korea for a while (as she has) and who 'just ignore some things and you just have to deal with it and roll with the punches'. According to Jessica,

(4) culturally it is quite different right, to be living here and actually seeing your mother-in-law and dealing with a lot of cultural different aspects. Things like going to funerals or having to deal with your husband's workplace culture... well for most of the ladies that are in the States they just don't have to deal with that right. I mean maybe they say something like 'oh, what is Thanksgiving called in Korea?' whereas the nitty gritty it is a little different. [Jessica, interview]

Her ideas about these different life experiences, and the way they will likely impact on the values and shared culture people will have, then shape her behaviour, in that they led her to leave one Facebook group that was based in the US in order to join one based in Korea. This then is a clear case of context design in the sense that she was able to exert an element of control over the way her posts were likely to be interpreted by constructing and then aligning with a group she felt shared her experiences and values.

An explicit awareness of the intradiverse context is also cited by many survey respondents as the reason for concerns they have about causing offence:

(5) of course, if you say something that every person you know will hear, it needs to be something you would say in front of every single one of them. swearing would upset my mum, liberal or conservative views would upset some friends, etc. [Q24-13]

Implied in the above is a projection on the part of the poster about how their different Friends may interpret what is said, presumably based on experience of their relationships with these people; so, the poster believes they know how their mother will respond to particular posts and how their friends will respond to others. In the following response, the focus is less on the different relationships represented in their Friends network, and instead on the respondent's understanding of the varied values held by potential readers of their Facebook posts; in other words, the more submerged and potentially complex elements that make up their intradiverse network:

(6) I have friends who are of different types. Some are more religious, some are more structured in their mindset, some have great senses of humor, some don't.....so, yeah, I do think about what I'm posting in terms of, who can see it, and what will they think. [Q24-15]

The above examples from the survey display some indication that posters are aware of the different segments of their audience (the 'different types of friends') and have some confidence in thus appropriately designing the context for the interpretation of their posts. Other respondents raise the issue that there is very little control over the possible audience, unlike in typical face-to-face situations, as seen for example in the following reference to the possibility of 'someone random' unexpectedly joining the discussion:

(7) I don't worry about accidentally offending someone, but I avoid posting things that I know will offend some people because I don't like offending people. I don't feel it's the best place to discuss different viewpoints due to its public nature and the very mixed audience who would be reading my posts. I would rather discuss different opinions in real life when someone random isn't likely to join in. [Q24-76]

As this example suggests, the potential audience for any post is consciously seen, by some posters at least, not only as intradiverse but also unpredictable ('random'), two features of Facebook networks which intersect in important ways: i.e. it is not possible to be sure who from the varied network that constitutes the audience will be reading any one of your posts (and which, depending on settings, may well include people beyond your immediate Friends list). The implication from the above (and other) responses is that the best way to deal with this situation is to frame the communication in a way that avoids offending anyone; that is, deliberately avoid debating 'different viewpoints' and instead actively and consciously design a context in which as many people as possible can favourably interpret the post. Thus we begin to see one way in which context design processes are shaped by users' awareness of, and responses to, intradiversity.

Having established users' awareness regarding intradiversity as a factor in context design, we move to looking at the types of issue that are reported as causing offence. As evident in the following list of what should be avoided on Facebook, people often appeared to have a complex and very specific ideology regarding what was a potential cause for offence.

(8) Food photos—everybody eats everyday and I don't need to share every meal in Instagram filtered photos. Relationships—prefer to keep public displays of affection to a minimum—nobody really needs nor wants to know how wonderful/awful etc my partner is. Illness—need to know basis—everyone gets ill so I wouldn't post about it as it implies I am looking for attention. Expression of emotions—e.g. Boredom/nerves/happiness/sadness etc.—it is a little narcissistic. Random 'selfies'—too narcissistic Political views—if I wanted to discuss politics, I would do it in person as too much ambiguity on fbk and i see fbk as a way for personal interactions/humour not a political forum. Work—leave work at 'the office door'—I use fbk for personal connections not employment related moans/rants/discussions etc. [Q17-113]

Below we categorise the often extensive and varied factors into the following categories: values and opinions one disagrees with; self-perception; misreading of context; and norms of online behaviour one disagrees with. These categories highlight the expectations that people have in terms of acceptable behaviour, and how this relates to the types of communication they feel Facebook is best suited to due to its affordances and the ideological assumptions they have towards it; the categories also indicate wider values and opinions about social, cultural and political issues, and beliefs about how these are handled in public interaction.

Before outlining the categories however it is worth saying a word about what is understood as offence in this context. We chose not to offer participants an up-front definition of the term as part of the questionnaire, so responses are deliberately based on how the participants themselves conceptualise the concept. The categories below show the range of issues that provoked offence, although people also talked of more minor issues which they saw as annoying rather than offensive: one respondent, for example, wrote that 'It doesn't offend me so much as annoy me if people don't verify facts'. As such issues were included in their responses to the questions, we categorise them here under the more general term 'offence', firstly because participants themselves chose to recount incidents which 'bothered' them or which they 'don't appreciate' in response to our question about offence; and because they also help indicate people's attitudes towards how Facebook is perceived as a communicative space. In other words, the data reports on issues that were identified as communicative offences by users, ranging from the seemingly trivial (which perhaps relates to the culture of inconsequentiality which exists on Facebook) to the more substantive.

Causes of Offence

Values and Opinions One Disagrees with

The overwhelming majority of the 60% had been offended by the expression of opinions, particularly religious or political ones, or by comments deemed sexist, racist or homophobic. This was the case in 69 of the 78 responses to the question of whether they had ever taken offence (Q. 26). Examples include:

(9) Generally I have been offended by fairly controversial posts (antiabortionism) and I usually just block the post. I don't see the value

in arguing within a Facebook post (it's not the best medium for real debate). [Q26-81]

(10) I remember defriending one person (friend of a friend) as she kept posting her political opinions that were the complete opposite of mine. ... It frustrated me as I didn't know her well enough to 'bite' and reply to her posts, equally, I didn't want to voice it on a public forum. So I decided the best thing to do was just to defriend her. [Q26-52]

People's awareness of intradiversity was instrumental in their apparent acceptance that conflicting opinions were to some extent inevitable, given their understanding of their wide circle of varied Friends. This was particularly the case where respondents were explaining why they might inadvertently offend others or why they avoided certain topics; and, as we shall see later, this acceptance was also important in explaining how and why they responded to being offended. In explaining what they would not post about, the following respondent claims to avoid controversial topics on the basis that 'it doesn't seem unlikely that somebody could take issue with what i post':

(11) negative comments about anybody who might [read] my posts; don't want them to see what I'm thinking. any opinions that might be controversial (politics, etc.); don't want to receive negative attention, and since I have such a wide range of Facebook friends, it doesn't seem unlikely that somebody could take issue with what i post. [Q17-51]

Different aspects of intradiversity are indexed by respondents to explain why conflicting opinions regarding politics and other matters might be such an issue on Facebook. To some respondents, the tribal aspect of social affiliations is cited as significant, where one's identity is indexed by aligning with, and equally disidentifying against, a particular group, be it political or sports related (as in the following examples). In these cases, intradiversity is conceptualised by participants in terms of their audience orienting to very salient political or cultural centres of authority or influence (a political party, a sports team):

(12) It [the issue over which the respondent caused offence] was a quiz result relating to the US election some years ago. A crazy Republican who had no problem going on and on about his views took offence

to the fact that I had a different view, had a hissy fit, and defriended me. Yes, over a quiz result. People are strange. [Q22-26]

(13) I made a joke about how terrible the Chicago Cubs are. The fans are a sensitive bunch, and this person unfriended me. [Q22-22]

In line with this view, there is also recognition across the responses that views about issues such as politics are often very strongly held, and thus lead to equally strong reactions. These are often seen as deeply embedded in people's value systems, and thus not open to debate. In response to the question of what they would not post about, two respondents said:

(14) Overly political things, because hoooo boy people can get their knickers in a twist over that. [Q17-55]

(15) Anything to do with religion or politics as I have quite strong views and you can't 'win'. [Q17-82]

However, there was also some recognition of the polycentricity of contemporary life, and the fact that people's affiliations are both multiple and shifting: they can orient (equally strongly) to more than one centre of influence simultaneously or move from one 'micro-hegemony' to the other (Blommaert and Varis 2013). Views may be strongly held, but they are nonetheless hard to predict in relation to specific debates or events. This was illustrated in our interview with Heather, who discovered many of her Friends' positions on the Scottish independence referendum of 2014 through Facebook:

(16) I think it is easy to presume everyone on your Facebook you are friends with has the same view and then... it was interesting around the time of the referendum because a lot of my friends back home had yes's and no's popping up at the side of their pictures, with different campaign logos on the side of their Facebook profile picture. [Heather, interview]

The following survey response also illustrates how one's Friends list may be seen as holding particularly varied, and unwelcome, views.

(17) Some 'friends' have had quite radical (in my opinion) views about religion and society. E.g. a girl I knew who was a very conservative

muslim, who would criticise Western culture a lot, and be spiteful towards people who did not share her views. And another girl who sympthised with the riots that happened [across the UK] a couple of years ago. I removed them both as friends—if their opinions could annoy me so much, I don't want to see them in my news-feed, particularly when we were just acquaintances. [Q26-41]

The fact that many of these connections can be unfriended without too much worry suggests that often such acquaintances constitute weak ties. The varied nature of the relationships one has on Facebook—from close to distant family, colleagues or connections from work, and the different spectrum of friendships and acquaintances—are another aspect of the intradiversity that constitutes these networks. The responsibilities one has in these different relationships is another factor in how people responded to different situations: as we shall see later, it was sometimes not felt possible for people to unfriend those with whom they had a closer relationship, or where they felt bound, for other social reasons, to maintain a visible link.

Intradiversity is also shown in the way that the different Friends of one Facebook user are described as relating to each other when brought together in the space of their mutual Friend's feed. That is, when connections from different parts of the poster's biography (and with whom they have different types of relation: e.g. friendship versus family-based relationship) are brought into dialogue. In such cases, the fact that the people involved do not know each other (and are linked only by their mutual relationship with the node user) may make them feel they have more freedom to be antagonistic in a way that they would not be with those they have close relationships with. The examples below mention this type of confrontation as they address what the respondent would not post about on Facebook (the first example) and whether they have ever offended anyone (the second).

(18) Vulgar things and things that are too political. I have previously posted something vaguely political but two of my friends who didn't know each other started a Facebook fight on my page. So I no longer touch that. [Q17-28]

(19) It was a political-religious issue and I was posting only to share the article, because it affected me. However, some people can't help but be rude and offensive to others, and one of my family

members attacked one of my friends, so I removed the post and the family member removed me from their friends. [Q22-13]

As well as recognising the intradiverse nature of the audience brought together on Facebook, other affordances of the site were suggested to explain the likelihood that conflicting opinions are likely to lead to offence in this communicative space. According to our survey, people on the whole do not feel that Facebook is the right forum for discussion of politics and other controversial or serious topics, as there is no room for real conversation. Implicit in this belief is the realisation that the online space does not allow a user to sufficiently frame their political statements or, in other words, to design the context in a way that will ensure an intended interpretation. There is also the suggestion that people may be more extreme on Facebook, and respond to political views in a way they would not in a face-to-face situation (and are therefore perhaps harder to predict or control). For example, this respondent would not post:

(20) Stuff that has to do with politics—I think it's kind of ridiculous how people get into really heated political debates on Facebook. I think people say things also, that they might not say if they were having the conversation in person. [Q17-120]

Likewise this respondent explains that:

(21) I very intentionally avoid posting about various political and religious topics for the following reasons (in no particular order): I don't want to be defined by a single specific comment or belief. I know I have friends that hold a wide range of views on a given topic (for instance, gun control). I don't want a disagreement about a certain issue to compromise a friendship. I don't think Facebook facilitates good dialogue, and I feel like political and religious topics deserve more than a single statement. There's no room for actual conversation, so if a comment needs conversation for context, I don't post it. [Q17-6]

In contrast, however, Heather's perception of Facebook (as outlined in her interview) was that the affordances of the written medium in fact encouraged more thoughtful and sustained debate:

(22) you have got more time to have a measured response ... I tend to be quite easily convinced by other people verbally whereas

on Facebook I was reading what this guy said and I didn't agree with him but I was like 'OK he has made a fair enough point but ...' and then had time to think of something to come back. [Heather, interview]

How people perceive the available affordances varies, and these varied perceptions encourage different kinds of behaviour—Heather suggests she has 'had several political discussions on Facebook' whereas a number of survey respondents claimed to avoid them.

There is also an awareness among some respondents that the potential permanence and unpredictable textual trajectory of online comments can also be a factor in this context, and that opinions one expresses now could be a problem in the future in as-yet-unanticipated circumstances. In other words, the *persistence* and *replicability* (boyd and Marwick 2011, p. 9) of online texts are factors shaping how people claim to act on Facebook. This is the process associated with a 'fear of entextualisation', as we mentioned in Chap. 2—the loss of control over a post's trajectory that people can experience when posting online. It is another example of context design, in which (one or more) imagined future scenarios are suggested as influencing a user's current practices.

(23) I don't often post my opinions about politics because most of my friends have different views and like to argue. I rarely post anything controversial in part because I know that I'll forget about it and I think it may come back to haunt me somehow. [Q17-125]

Interestingly, at the same time, the speed at which the Facebook newsfeed changes is also cited as a reason for not worrying about offences caused. In explaining why he had not rectified an offence online, our interviewee Jacob explained: 'Facebook things keep flying on so quickly. You can't find one message that was posted on one day so I think it is kind of too late now to undo my damage'.

According to many of our respondents, then, politics and other potentially contentious issues are best avoided on Facebook, in part because of the intradiverse nature of the Friend network and the issues this may cause given the perception that the site's affordances mitigate against reasoned debate. Of the 53 people who answered the question about what constituted a typical status update (Q. 14), only nine explicitly included politics as a topic they *did* post about. Despite the general feeling that politics and other controversial subjects should be avoided, it is important not to ignore the handful that claimed to talk about politics and for whom, in fact, it figured as an important part of their identity presentation. This is important because these responses show that, despite the overwhelming feeling that political discussion is not an appropriate function for the site, many people are clearly using it as a place to air political views:

(24) My typical status update is about an important event or something happened during the day that really surprised me and I would like to share with my friends on Facebook. Mostly they are about political events and news. [Q14-141]

(25) I often post things that make me laugh or I think make my friend have a laugh. Sometimes I also post comments on recent news, usually on politics or sports. [Q14-127]

(26) Share my achievements and promote charity or political causes I care about. [Q14-62]

The fact that politics was singled out as a topic which caused offence shows its salience on the site (despite people's dislike of it), and we will return to examine this contradiction further when we discuss the strategies people use to avoid being offended, and what this indicates about the type of community they are constructing on the site.

Self-perception

In many of the responses, the offence centred around the person's sense of self, or the self they wished to project. If being offended is a discursively-enacted stance, as we discussed in Chap. 3, then such stance-taking can be seen as part of the processes of disidentification in which our respondents engaged on the site (Leppänen et al. 2014). Responses of this sort involved personal misunderstandings, posts deemed to be insulting, or those which violated the respondent's privacy in various ways. The three below, for example, mention being tagged in photos they disapproved of; the public airing of a matter they deemed to be private; and feeling a loss of control over their newsfeed.

(27) Someone of the opposite sex tagged me in a picture with herself, which caused many of my friends to think that it was my girlfriend

(it was not). I asked her to untag me and that was pretty much it, although I had to personally reply to several people telling them she was in fact not my girlfriend. [Q26-20]

(28) My sister posted a very unflattering picture of me and tagged me in it. [Q26-32]

(29) I am generally worried about what people post about me on Facebook. As I know that we are not all very sensitive on the concept of privacy I do not want people to share information or pictures of me that I would not share on facebook. [Q26-60]

In these examples, it is the interpretation the other will have about one's self-image that causes anxiety, which may be exacerbated by the large and semi-public nature of the possible audience for the posts. Their concerns can be seen as linked to processes of authentication, and the desire to project an individual identity that has an essential consistency, a notion which can be challenged by the 'networked' nature of online identity; that is, by the fact that people's online identity is shaped not only by their own actions but by contributions made by others in their network and by the expectations of different friendship groups (boyd 2012). Evident across the above responses is the feeling that the user is willing to work to ensure that others do not contradict or mar their self-presentation (see also McLaughlin and Vitak 2011). The last example also suggests an awareness on the part of the respondent regarding people's different attitudes to the use of Facebook (as a fully public forum versus something semi-public or contained), which also indicates a diversity of opinion in terms of values.

Respondents' awareness of the networked nature of identification processes on Facebook is also evident in their attempts not to violate the privacy of others:

(30) I also avoid posting too many personal pictures (especially together with other people as to protect their privacy), etc. [Q17-11]

Again, as in boyd's (2012) work, the Facebook users in our survey have some awareness of the implications of networked privacy; the fact that privacy online is often not a case of an individual's control over information flows, but of how information is managed within and beyond their personal network. In her interview, Jessica explained how she had warned her Facebook group about a blogger who wanted to join, on the grounds of concerns about the blogger's privacy norms—'her personal filter is a little bit different than what I perceived the group would want'. However, Jessica's actions were seen by members of the group who knew the woman personally as breaching etiquette norms, which they took exception to. The fact that Jessica then left the group for another can be seen as an act of context design, in the sense that the future security breaches she imagined might take place if the woman joined the group (and which she had tried to explain to the group in order to shape their immediate behaviour) led her to change the immediate context in which she interacted.

Returning to the notion of self-perception, particular attention is thus paid both to the persona the poster him/herself wishes to present, given the intradiverse nature of the network, and to the rights of others in this respect. For example, in the following there is an awareness of the way their interaction might affect other people, as well as the dynamic of the different relationships they have on Facebook. Asked about what they would not post the respondent replied:

(31) Personal Problems—Many of my Facebook "friends" aren't friends in real life, so I don't want to share this sort of personal information. Gossip/rumors, information that might be hurtful to another person. [Q17-9]

The concerns here are based on an awareness of what 'friend' means in this context, and that many of their online connections are with acquaintances who the respondent would not consider to be close relationships (i.e. friends in a traditional understanding of the word).

As the above suggests, there was indication of an awareness among our participants of the discursive nature of identity, and the fact that this can enable the deliberate construction of a positive persona. The discursive construction of identity is well-documented in sociolinguistic studies, and our research points to the fact that people are very aware not only of processes of identification, but also the need to conduct different identity performances in different contexts (see also Tagg and Seargeant 2017). The following respondent, for example, likens self-presentation on Facebook to a kind of public relations work:

(32) On Facebook people, myself included, mostly seem to want to post about positive things because you are presenting your public face to an audience of people you know well and also to some people you haven't seen for 15 years and wouldn't speak to if you passed them on the street. You are in control of your public imagine on Facebook, you're your own PR officer and most people want that imagine to be positive. [Q17-60]

The other side of the coin is the sense that Facebook is being *overly* used for types of self-promotion by others, which, if one's friendship is not of a very close nature, can be perceived as annoying.

(33) I wrote to a friend about how my 2 year old was counting to 40 and was saying the alphabet in 3 languages. This made a FB contact write passive aggressively on her wall about overachieving parents who spend all their time bragging about their children. I felt the need to defriend her after that incident. Another former classmate complained in a status update about not wanting to see people's kids on FB because they were annoying pictures, so I defriended her too. [Q22-16]

What these examples highlight is how closely processes of context design are linked to (dis)identification processes, to people's attempt to project a particular kind of identity and to participate in the identity projects of others. In framing their posts to be interpreted in particular ways, users are driven in part by their conscious desire for their performed identity to be recognised and authenticated by others.

Misreading of Context

Another intradiversity-related issue concerns the way posts are interpreted because of the varied nature of the possible contexts in which they are read and the fact that the original or intended context can be lost or 'misread'. This is voiced, for example, with reference to experiences where a supposedly humorous comment fell flat. In instances such as this, the fact that the online space makes it harder for a comment to be framed as humorous—because, that is, people cannot draw on contextualisation cues such as tone of voice or winking and smiling—means it is easier for such misinterpretations to take place:

(34) A friend of mine organised a farewell party for me when I was about to leave the UK. Another fellow Singaporean made a nasty remark which he thought was a funny joke perhaps, saying that 'it's okay that she's leaving the UK, the cooler Singaporean is still around'. It offended because that seemed like an insult to me. I told this to the party organiser, who dropped a note to that Singaporean saying that that wasn't very nice. He came to apologise as a result. [Q26-53]

(35) I have a coworker from Alaska and I am from MN. I boasted that in MN we do cooler activities in the cold cold weather. She took offence that I was offending AK. I wrote to her that I was trying to be cute by being competitive about our cold weather that other people hate. She acknowledged that she over reacted. [Q22-7]

There was also evidence of people having an explicit awareness of this; that is, of the way the lack of contextualisation cues might cause problems. The respondent in the following suggests that the 'meaning can get lost when written down', yet claims to repeat the behaviour nonetheless. The implication is that communication on Facebook is intended to be trivial and amusing, and that miscommunications are neither surprising nor problematic.

(36) I'm sure I offend lots of people. Most the time it's just a joke but the meaning can get lost when written down. Normally a sorry and rewording of the phrase sorts it out. [Q22-42]

There are also incidents where it is not so much the lack of contextualisation cues as more generalised difference of opinion as to what counts as humour. In instances like this the affordances of the site are less the issue, than the fact that the intradiverse audience brings together people with different values around humour.

(37) i was taking the piss out of a bald bloke on his profile picture - me and one of his other friends were posting funny pictures and making quips about his head - and he went bonkers and PMed me lots of abusive, aggressive stuff. I defriended him, i dont want genuine abuse on facebook, just light-hearted piss-taking [Q22-10]

Of course, while this respondent appears to interpret the incident in terms of different ideas about humour, it is difficult to evaluate this interpretation without access to the interactions in question; what for one person is seen as 'taking the piss' is for another 'abusive, aggressive stuff'. This is a point that underlies all our data: the fact that people tend to portray others' actions as offensive, while explaining instances where they were deemed to have offended others as indicative of the different values on the site or of others misreading their intentions.

Differences in how people evaluate a situation—given the distance afforded by virtual communication and the inevitable recontextualisation of posts—was also evident in Heather's in-depth account in interview of what happened when she updated her status with her reaction to an earlier encounter with a fox. According to her account, she had come home one evening to find that a fox had tipped over her dustbin, leaving her to clear up the rubbish from the road. It was 'absolutely vile' and so when she was finished she went to her computer to write the following status update on Facebook, as recalled in interview: 'I absolutely hate foxes, they are an absolute nightmare and they have just turned over the rubbish'. Almost immediately she started receiving offended and seemingly aggressive comments, pointing out such things as 'you have destroyed their natural habitat, what do you expect them to do' and 'we need to protect the foxes'. According to Heather, she 'couldn't believe' that what she saw as such as trivial post about foxes had caused such offence. She describes the 'awkward tension' between herself and one of the women she offended when they next met, and reports on their mutual friends' response:

(38) We were in a group of people and then she left quite early, she didn't hang around to chat with us and I just thought I really hope that is not because of the fox conversation. My other friends thought it was absolutely hilarious that we couldn't talk about the situation and was like be an adult and go over and say something and I am like what am I supposed to say? 'I am really sorry I offended you with my comment about foxes?' [Heather, interview]

The misreadings of context discussed in this section may rest on the particular nature of the relationships that a poster has with different people in their network. That is, context is perhaps more likely to be misread where the people involved are not close acquaintances. This was a reason suggested by Heather, who felt that a shared background was instrumental on Facebook, given that the mediated nature of communication as well as the lack of contextualisation cues could otherwise lead people to interpret her posts—like the one above about the fox—in ways that she did not intend.

(39) on Facebook I feel I can put things ...because people know me they will be like 'oh yes that is the sort of thing Heather would say.' .... if people know me really well they would know how I would say it and respect me for saying it whereas in that situation it just lost me friends. [Heather, interview]

Norms of Behaviour One Disagrees with

Expectations concerning the norms that are deemed acceptable, both in public discourse generally and specifically for Facebook as a communicative space, were another source of offence.

(40) Had a friend who came out and revealed he is gay by posting videos and pictures of naked men which come on my news feed. Don't appreciate a video of naked men playing automatically on my news feed. Stopped following him as a result. [Q26-62]

(41) It was a picture of a ducks genetalia... posted as a joke in reference to a private offline conversation. Some people commented that they disliked the image and I untagged myself. No further reaction took place after this point. [Q22-41]

(42) One of my friends lent me a book, and was unhappy about the condition when I gave it back. But instead of actually saying something about it, he complained about it on facebook. I gave him a new copy, but things were never really okay between us after that. [Q26-1]

As one can see from the above examples, these range from issues that might be considered problematic in many 'public' contexts (pictures of nudity), to behaviour specific to the channel via which the communication is effected (the use of the semi-public space of a Facebook interaction for what is considered a personal dispute). An example of the latter kind of issue was also provided by one of the interviewees, Jacob, who explained what happened when he did not respond to his wife's post announcing her pregnancy:

(43) she came to me, at I guess at the end of the day after she had posted it, and said 'why didn't you like my post?' and I said 'well, I kind of decided like, in terms of we are husband and wife, we don't need to communicate like that'. ... I guess the way that she viewed my role... her view of my role on Facebook I think was different from my, what I thought my role is... [Jacob, interview]

The offence Jacob caused by not Liking his wife's post came about from their very different expectations about what constitutes appropriate behaviour on Facebook (as well as the role that Facebook should play within their relationship), and it illustrates how behavioural norms are being continually negotiated on (and off) the site.

In many instances, the expectations regarding appropriate norms relate to seemingly trivial things but, as noted above, these are still a response to the question of what people were offended by, and thus indicate the different extremes of behaviour which people react to as they construct the ideal of how they see Facebook as a communicative space. One respondent, for example, claimed to be offended by:

(44) Games posts, my girlfriend left me posts. Usually I block them. [Q26-59]

Another source of contention is differing interpretations of what counts as humour, or what is considered acceptable for satiric remark. The following two examples both involve light-hearted treatment of figures who were involved in tragic events: in the first, Gary Glitter, the British pop star convicted of paedophilia; in the second Mary Jo Kopechne, the woman who died in a car accident with Ted Kennedy:

(45) I posted that I had entertained my middle school students with a 70s video of Gary Glitter singing some hit of the time. The point was they had laughed at the clothes and hair, but someone I was close to got very offended (he had been accused of child sexual abuse by that point.) We fell out for a long time, and it was a nasty episode. I rarely post such things now as I always think about who may be offended. [Q22-3]

(46) Made a Mary Jo Kopechne joke when Ted Kennedy died in 2009.

(47) Someone told me the post was offensive as it was tasteless and insensitive. I eventually pulled down the post. [Q22-39]

On occasions, the sensitivities that one is falling foul of are not ones that one might appreciate oneself initially. In the following example, the poster uses the word 'uppity', not realising that its collocations during the slave era have given it a particular derogatory meaning in certain cultural contexts.

(48) I used the word "uppity". I did not realise that this word has racist connotation. [Q22-19]

Importantly, beliefs about what others do affect what people say they will not do themselves. Our respondents talk, for example, of what they themselves find boring or annoying, projecting these as issues other people would likewise find annoying, and thus adapt their own behaviour accordingly. This was raised by the following respondent as they listed what they would not post about on Facebook:

(49) Problems with/complaints about my husband (good recipe for marital discord!) Complaints/passive-aggressive comments about other people (I don't want to be that kind of person) Things that other people see too much of on their news feed (food pictures, complaints about weather or sports teams, too many baby updates) Stuff that no one cares about (I'm bored today, I really want a strawberry daquiri, I am having a bad hair day). [Q17-2]

In this and the following examples, the logic is based on an idea of what they themselves do *not* wish their own online personas to resemble, based in turn on their experiences of those of others. In other words, a process of disidentification with behaviours exhibited by others, and a sense of their own identity, emerges from their experiences and their awareness of some kind of group identity from which they want to differentiate themselves. Triviality, or excessively personal issues, are often cited in this context, suggesting that the persona the respondents are keen to avoid is one which is seen as overly superficial, or not sensitive to the public nature of the space (and who therefore indulges in very personal observations):

(50) Other things I wouldn't post about are trivial news or topics everybody is already talking about. I hate when everybody in my news feed is talking about the same topics and feeds are repetitive and boring, especially if the topic is a trivial one. [Q17-132]

(51) bowel movements, sex, and other things I don't talk to casual acquaintances about offline. I might make an exception if I think I have something very funny to say. Food I've made or eaten. I've noticed that a lot of people find this kind of post annoying, so I avoid it. [Q17-42]

(52) politics, sex, very private thoughts and events, anything that might offend people Two reasons for this: firstly, I don't like to live my private life on FCB; secondly, I don't like to read this kind of stuff on my news feed so naturally I don't post it myself. [Q24-76]

The idea that respondents hold themselves to the same standards as others is often mentioned. In reply to the question of what they would not post about, this respondent answered:

(53) Nothing politically controversial – professional etiquette I never forward round robin posts/emails… they really annoy me in my own timeline and assume the same for most others. [Q17-15]

This is often coupled with a general motivation to come across in a positive light; and to ensure that their persona is not a product of a litany of postings they are critical of when they appear in their own newsfeed:

(54) Family conflict. Or daily challenges/bad days/complaints. Why? It's annoying when people continually complain about things. Now, I don't mind if they're venting once in awhile. And I don't mind them posting/sharing in a group, and am always supportive there. But it's annoying when someone's always venting on their own wall about negative stuff. [Q17-24]

Elsewhere we have argued that, in terms of the social roles people orient to on Facebook, the idea of a positive persona is foundational (Tagg and Seargeant 2017), which accords with the idea that people for the most part put forward their 'best' selves in the identity they construct on Facebook (Baron 2007; McLaughlin and Vitak 2011). To the extent that a positive identity involves not annoying or offending others (by avoiding posts that they themselves find annoying in others), it is evident again that identity construction plays a key role in how context is designed on Facebook.

Summary

In this chapter, we outline the main categories of what people report as finding offensive, and what they often therefore say they try to avoid doing themselves so not as to cause offence. In terms of intradiversity, our participants' responses highlight the range and variety of worldviews and expectations that may be found, particularly at the periphery of one's online network (made up, as it is, by both close and weak ties from across one's biography); and the fact that this diversity may manifest itself in relation to political and religious views, as well as ideas regarding communicative norms and appropriate behaviour, both on Facebook specifically and more generally in 'public' forums. It can also be made relevant through personal misunderstanding (itself aggravated by intradiversity) and misreadings of context, which are exacerbated by the nature of online encounters. Central to people's acts of offence-taking is the process of online (dis)identification, and the desire to construct—and have authenticated—a particular kind of identity. The networked nature of intradiverse audiences on sites like Facebook also means that identification and privacy management must be seen not as an individual endeavour (as traditionally conceptualised) but as a collective act, involving negotiation and shared responsibility within the network, and that people are constantly positioning themselves in relation to the behaviour of others and their perceived evaluation of it. What this data begins to show, then, is the way in which communication on Facebook is shaped by users' awareness—and sometime misreading—of the more implicit and submerged values which both emerge from, and define, an intradiverse network. These findings, and our concept of intradiversity, have important implications for a scholarly understanding of how contemporary patterns of diversity manifest themselves, and how they constrain and structure behaviour and our relationships with others.

In terms of what this discussion tells us about context design, we have seen that people's awareness of their intradiverse audience shapes the decisions they make regarding what to post on Facebook in various ways. People say they tend to avoid politics and other issues which they deem controversial given their awareness of the potentially varied views held by their Friends; they are careful not to post information or pictures which might violate the self-presentation or privacy of their online contacts; and many of them consciously avoid posting trivial, negative or inappropriate contributions which they themselves object to seeing in their newsfeed. Importantly, we have seen how context design is often reactive, in the sense that people's postings are shaped by their experience of, and response to, others' behaviour, and that it is closely linked to processes of (dis)identification, as individuals seek to frame their posts in ways that contribute to the particular persona they are trying to convey.

We also begin to see here how context design draws on sometimes quite elaborate ideas about possible future scenarios, based on people's perceptions regarding the likely trajectories of their posts. Again, this crucial aspect of the process is particularly evident in the interview data. Jessica, for example, who is pregnant, is aware that posts concerning her baby will add to his 'digital footprint' and 'as he gets older he doesn't need one created by us right?' This stated viewpoint is very much grounded in current privacy fears surrounding sites like Facebook which may well have changed by the time her child is older. So she is projecting current norms or ideologies onto the future; and tailoring her current behaviour accordingly. She herself shows some explicit awareness of this, saying elsewhere that 'Later on I may not care but I would still like to have some sort of control'. Heather, meanwhile, comments specifically on the potential for her posts to be accessed at the school where she works, and uses this as a constraint on her posting behaviour: 'if I go to post something I think "worst case scenario—if one of my kids or my headteacher saw this or my line manager, would I be able to explain my way out of it?"'

Finally, we have also pointed to an apparent contradiction between people's perception of the site as trivial, fun and not the place for serious debate (which apparently guides the way they design the context for their postings) and the fact that the site is clearly being used for political discussion by many people. This point, which we return to later, suggests that people's stated ideas about what a site is for may not always match the purposes for which they—or others—are actually using it. In the next chapter, however, we move to a discussion of what emerges as a general trend across the participants in terms of the type of space and environment they see Facebook ideally operating as.

CHAPTER 6

Constructing Conviviality in Online Interaction

Abstract Drawing in detail on the findings of the study, this chapter argues that *online conviviality*—the desire for peaceful co-existence through negotiating or ignoring difference and avoiding contentious debate—is an overarching principle for this particular type of social media encounter. This has significant implications for our understanding of how people manage their social interactions and their performance of identity in this kind of online context, and, by extension, our understanding of contemporary social relations. The results reveal that, for this ego-centred network of users at least, attitudes towards difference (in terms of opinion, attitude and ideological stance) stop short of any deep engagement with opposing political views or social practices, which indicates that in this case users' perception of Facebook as a convivial space is unlikely to encourage the sort of mutual engagement and understanding across cultural, political and social boundaries which was imagined in the early days of the internet.

Keywords Agency · Difference · Conviviality · Positive persona

CONVIVIALITY AND THE POSITIVE PERSONA

Having explored in the last chapter the kinds of posts which cause offence, in this chapter, we again draw on the data from the survey to examine how people respond to instances of offending or being offended, and what sort of general pattern can be perceived from this in terms of the media ideologies people have about Facebook and the type of interactive space they construct it as. Specifically, we look at how the way they choose to respond appears to be shaped in part by the desire to establish and/or maintain a sense of civility within their network and in the communicative space of Facebook.

As we saw in the previous chapter, the intradiverse nature of people's networks, along with the different social expectations that come with the maintenance of different types of relationships, meant that there was a guardedness to what people posted or how they posted it. A motivating factor behind how they managed their online communication was a reluctance to provoke conflict; in the response below, for example, this is ultimately presented as paramount, even if it means compromising on a stated commitment to displaying what is put across as an authentic self:

(55) I don't say anything [on Facebook] I don't believe fundamentally, so if someone is offended by that, we're probably not really friends to begin with. I'd rather just delete the person. Exception: things that would offend my parents. And I do avoid talking about religion (I'm an atheist) because my uncle is a pastor, with whom I disagree very strongly. I don't mind other religions or anything, but I really hate the politics of his particular branch. I don't want to start a blood feud or something. [Q14-82]

Responses such as this, and others we analyse below, suggest that what we call 'online conviviality' is an overarching principle shaping relations and behaviour on Facebook. The term 'conviviality' stems as a theoretical concept from discussions of civility, and has its origins in descriptions of superdiverse neighbourhoods, in the context of which diversity has become 'commonplace' (Wessendorf 2014a, b) or normalised (Gilroy 2004). In superdiverse situations, where 'almost everybody comes from elsewhere' (as one of the inner city London residents in Wessendorf's 2014a study puts it, p. 398) and where people's origins are often neither straightforward nor obvious, it may be necessary for people to overlook difference in order to conduct their public lives normally (Wessendorf 2014a, p. 398). In these situations, civility is often used as a strategy for the avoidance of conflict through striking a fine balance between acknowledging difference and keeping a distance. Civility has been described as a main 'interactional principle' in public superdiverse spaces, by which participants faced by visible displays of difference 'act in a civil manner' (Lofland 1989: 464 or 465). In Buonfino and Mulgan's (2009) conception, it is described as a 'learned grammar of sociability', and though based on the existing dispositions, something that is cultivated for the purposes of workable community relations.

Civility does not, however, necessarily imply an acceptance of difference, but may emerge simply from the desire to avoid tensions or as an indication of indifference. Wessendorf (2015, p. 8) writes that

> Underlying the skills necessary to communicate with people who differ in terms of their educational, ethnic, religious or class background is what has also been described as 'civility towards diversity' ... civility towards diversity does not necessarily imply a specific appreciation of diversity, but it means treating people universally the same, and it can emerge from indifference to diversity rather than form a specific appreciation of it.

The extent to which it can lead to deeper, more meaningful relationships and interactions is contentious, with some researchers finding that regular interactions facilitated friendships (Noble 2009; Wise 2007) and others warning that civility in public spaces may only mask continuing prejudices voiced at home (Valentine 2008, 2014). Wessendorf (2014a, b) paints a more complex picture, in which people use civility to ensure boundaries and where they avoid engaging with difference in order to enhance what they can obtain from their social relationships. She found, for example, that an ethnically diverse group of mothers spent their coffee mornings discussing issues of shared interest while cultural differences were acknowledged ('listened to') but not discussed. It is this complex understanding of how people exploit civility as an interactional strategy that is captured in the term 'conviviality'.

Using this notion as a starting point, we can see how the ways in which people negotiate the intradiverse networks they operate within on Facebook likewise calls for an accommodation of difference, which becomes a key element underpinning the contexts they design through their online interactions. As discussed in the previous chapter, a key theme that was voiced by many of the participants was the idea that the persona people portray online should be likeable, should avoid offending or annoying others, and should generally be considered in a positive light (Tagg and Seargeant 2017). The following response reflects how many participants described their typical status update:

(56) Positive things that have happened or good things I am feeling. I rarely post negative things or rants because people don't like seeing that and it makes me feel uncomfortable to share bad things that way. [Q14-3]

In terms of the space that these sorts of context design processes are aimed at producing then, the ideological identity that is being created for Facebook is one which, in the words of the following respondent, is generally 'fun'.

(57) I try really hard not to offend people on FB, not because it worries me, but because I think it makes it less fun. [Q24-28]

As we noted in the previous chapter, identity construction of this sort is seen as deliberate ('You are in control of your public image on Facebook') and also reactive, with users disidentifying with certain behaviours, and thus endeavouring to refrain from doing those particular things themselves. As one respondent explains after listing a number of things they wouldn't post, 'My reasons are that I find it annoying when others do this so it would be hypocritical of me to do it'. This was a common sentiment, and the way in which people purposefully mould their behaviour to the type of space they would like Facebook to be is a clear illustration of the context design process.

(58) I also try to keep my updates positive, so even if I'm having a bad day, I don't vent or be overly dramatic on FB. I think it's annoying when other people do that. [Q17-120]

If positivity and fun is a general aim, then conversely so is avoiding negativity, which again is a response to projections about who might be reading and the reaction they may have.

(59) Basically I try to keep any negativity off my wall, and I try to avoid anything I wouldn't want strangers to know about me (even though I keep my privacy settings pretty high), and I especially don't want my mother to worry about me. [Q17-119]

In this case, the concern is both for how his/her posts may be read by people with whom s/he has a very superficial relationship, but also people with very close relations (particularly his or her mother). The response is therefore interesting in highlighting how the desire to avoid conflict is shaped by people's awareness of the very different relationships they have with their Friends: in this case, the imagined reaction of their mother (presumably a strong tie) is the main concern, but the respondent is also careful not to reveal too much to those at the periphery of their network.

As discussed earlier, the construction of a broadly likeable identity which is designed to be accepted across an intradiverse audience can be seen as an attempt to avoid conflict emerging from difference (in, for example political views or ideas about acceptable behaviour). The desire to avoid difference is a key element of conviviality by which these Facebook users (in analogy with practices described in superdiverse neighbourhoods) seek to overlook potential sources of conflict in order to go about the business of interacting on Facebook. In this sense, creating a positive persona can be seen as a way of acting in a 'civil manner' (Lofland 1998, p. 29) which is appropriate to the particular communicative space of Facebook. As we explore below in our discussion of actions taken in response to instances of offence, the flipside of this may be that Facebook becomes a place, where discussion of more meaningful issues is considered out of place. When offence occurs, the strategies people use are mostly about smoothing over the issues rather than confronting them directly. People's responses to offensive posts were in the main also fairly laid-back in the sense that they explicitly comment on the fact that the offence is 'benign', and they seem to express a great deal of confidence in knowing how to deal with the situation. As one respondent put it:

(60) I don't care to have my newsfeed bombarded with game requests, religious material, whining or attention seeking stuff. But I'm not that fussed about it, I don't mind hiding them from my newsfeed, it's not that hard go change the settings. [Q26-57]

ACTIONS IN RESPONSE TO FEELINGS OF OFFENCE

The issue of how people deal with behaviour they find offensive for the various reasons listed in the previous chapter is instructive in terms of how they manage the intradiverse nature of the audience in order to maintain this sense of conviviality, and how they thus construct a particular context for their communication. The ways in which people deal with such situations also indicate their awareness of the affordances of Facebook, the nature of their relationships with people in their network, and the media ideologies that govern their beliefs about how the site is to be used. In this section, we itemise the various different categories of action people report taking, and discuss what this indicates about the way they design the context for their communication.

Blocking Posts

A first tactic reported was to block posts from people whose opinions or behaviour they regularly found offensive, so that these no longer showed up in their feed. As a tactic this was employed against people with whom respondents still wanted or needed to retain some element of a relationship—or at least not explicitly acknowledge that they no longer wished to interact (when one blocks someone that person is not notified that you have done this, and you maintain the connection within your network)—thus avoiding potential ill will. At the same time, by blocking them they were able to have control over their own experience of Facebook.

(61) I know someone who posts quite racist comments. I cannot defriend her so have simply adjusted things so I never see her posts. [Q26-2]

(62) Usually it is with facebook friends that I need to be friends with to keep the peace at work. They tend to be very conservative Christians with very dichotomous from my ideology etc. Um I usually just ask to unsubscribe from their posts. [Q26-9]

The example immediately above illustrates how it is the intradiverse nature of the network which prompts the issue, but that for convivial or social duty reasons (in this case in order to maintain their persona as a positive member of the workplace community) they are unable to break the ties, so instead simply mute them. In other words, blocking posts is often presented as an action appropriate for dealing with members of an intradiverse network with whom the respondent has a close, or complex, relationship. In the example above, the problem lies in the wider offline relationships the respondent has with the Friends, and his/her awareness of the norms and expectations of their shared workplace.

The decision between blocking or unfollowing (which amount to the same action) and unfriending (which we will come to in the next section) is explained in the following response in terms of the way that Facebook operates as a means of aligning oneself to a community for social reasons (in this case to avoid the social isolation that living abroad can lead to) in relatively superficial ways or for pragmatic reasons, but that these ties are far weaker than they would be with close friends. In order to balance the desire to maintain convivial relationships but not to have them lead to sources of potential conflict or frustration, hiding a feed is a preferable option to cutting the link altogether.

(63) This is terrible to say but if it is someone that I 'need' (boss, former boss, employment connection) I used to unfriend them but now I generally 'unfollow' or hide their news feed so that I don't need to see it. I'm an ELT [English language teaching] instructor, married to a Korean, so the community here is transient and I feel like I need to try to make some more permanent friends if only because they have more experience navigating the culture and have specific information that makes life here simpler. I feel guilty knowing that I most likely couldn't get through a meal with many of these people but at the same time the social isolation, plus lack of information isn't helping me either. [Q26-25]

Unfriending People

This careful consideration regarding the implications of actions taken on Facebook not only for online conviviality but also for wider relationships and other areas of people's lives is also suggested in the following post, in which 'a relative who has different political values' is blocked while other people are unfriended when their views or values are considered particularly offensive (homophobic, and related to neo-Nazi sentiments). The respondent was responding to the question that asked him about what offended him on Facebook.

(64) An elementary school friend posted neo-Nazi remarks. I unfriended him. [Q26-23]

(65) Political things that I don't agree with, particularly negative posts about Obama, or against homosexuality. I have unfriended homophobic people, and turned off posts from a relative who has different political values. [Q26-15]

Other answers were less clear as to what acted as the dividing line between blocking and unfriending, with either being used as a way to avoid interaction with views—mostly those of a political nature—which were considered offensive. In the following examples, however, it is evident that even posts framed as highly contentious (misogynist, radical, nationalistic) are met with a relatively discreet response, rather than a confrontation of any kind:

(66) A sexist, misogynist post really pissed me off, so I hid it. A post defending a terrible employer meant unfriending that individual. [Q26-18]

(67) radical/militant politics, racism, sexism, feminism, nationalism; very private info and photos; any kind of rude posts; explicit sexual posts. I hide such posts or even de-friend people. [Q26-11]

(68) American nationalistic b.s. and a friend consistently posting about conspiracy theories and tagging me in the posts. They got their feed blocked, or unfriended. [Q26-10]

As shown in the following post, for one person the decision about which cause of action to take was something which required difficult reflection, in part because s/he was having to monitor the communicative space—and thus the expectations and values of others—in his/her role as a moderator for a parents' forum. In this case, the diversity of norms of behaviour and of beliefs about etiquette are something that are filtered through the person of the moderator. Through decisions about how to deal with the different types of posts which can and do cause offence, the moderator designs the parameters for the context in which discussion takes place. In reply to what they found offensive on Facebook, this respondent replied:

(69) People posting offensive updates about parents, parents who overly judge other parents, and people who post racist or anti-religious views. I'm also a moderator for a parents forum, so we have to deal with a lot of people being offended about other people's posts. It is a daily discussion whether to leave/warn/or ban people for offensive posts/posts which people feel are offensive. [Q26-21]

The weak ties discussed above—which allowed for acts of defriending (in that nothing of great value is lost socially by cutting these ties)—are also cited as an option in some cases for a slightly different reason: because the relationship is not secure enough that it was felt it could sustain robust interaction. It was considered socially easier simply to drop the connection, than to engage with it on the topics of disagreement.

(70) I can't remember any solid examples [of being offended] but I do remember defriending one person (friend of a friend) as she kept posting her political opinions that were the complete opposite of mine. I wouldn't have minded too much as a lot of people post political opinions, but it came up on my news feed several times a week. It frustrated me as I didn't know her well enough to 'bite' and reply to her posts, equally, I didn't want to voice it on a public forum. So I decided the best thing to do was just to defriend her. [Q26-52]

A move similar to unfriending someone is to leave a Facebook group. Our interviewee Jessica did so on at least two occasions in response to instances of offence, according to the account she gave in her interview: first, the aforementioned argument over the female blogger and her privacy concerns; and, second, over an argument about endangered birds. In neither case did the group members appear to be close to her, and leaving the group was presented as fairly straightforward and unproblematic.

Ignoring Offending Posts

The majority of responses suggested that most people's response was to ignore the offending post(s). Asked what they got offended by, and what they did in response, the respondent below said:

(71) a. Their political views?—nothing b. Disturbing images (crime scene)—nothing [Q26-13]

The issue of the extent to which Facebook is an appropriate place to discuss politics is often given as a reason for why people prefer to avoid rather than engage in debate:

(72) Politics, because an online forum is not the right place for a thoughtful, considerate conversation [Q17-8]

As we saw in the previous chapter, this is given as a reason even when the topics are ones people feel strongly about:

(73)   I have a particularly hard time with pro-gun posts. I lived in Tucson, Arizona when Gabriel Giffords and several others were shot (some killed) in a supermarket parking lot. I had a friend commit suicide with his father's gun. I really, really wish guns were significantly less accessible and less glorified in American culture. Still, I don't think Facebook is really the place that people chose to listen to opposing views, so I usually ignore posts of that nature. I have unfriended at least one person after excessive posts on the topic. [Q26-4]

The following person expresses a similar scepticism about engaging with offensive posts, suggesting that confrontation and argument in this arena achieves very little, so is not worth the effort. Again, this shows how users imagine the likely contexts in which their posts will be interpreted (in this case, that they will be dismissed as 'over-reacting') which in turn shapes what they say:

(74)   One friend periodically posts broad generalizations about why people of certain nationalities are stupid or annoying. Sometimes I consider posting responses, but I know my offense will be seen as over-reacting and have no effect, so I don't bother. [Q26-6]

In order to have to avoid engaging with people she has offended, Jessica exploits the affordances of Facebook by changing the settings so that she is not alerted when anyone responds to her posts: 'I write my comment and I turn off the notifications because I just can't be bothered. Every once in a while I will check out of curiosity to see if somebody liked my post (laughs), because you know, you need that gratification'.

Underlying such opinions is the belief that Facebook is instead better suited to trivial or inconsequential matters, and as such is a fairly bland sort of entertainment rather than forum for serious debate:

(75)   an example is people posting their views about circumcision being wrong. i didnt get involved because i dont want to air my own views on important things on facebook—i dont think facebook is the place for deep or meaningful debate, it's for pictures of funny things and looking at people when bored. [Q26-14]

Its lack of seriousness is also felt to be a product of the lack of rigour with which information is chosen and circulated. Although we did not raise this in our survey, such assessments (which occurred across the dataset) speak to a growing public awareness of the problem of 'fake news' on Facebook and the ease with which false or inaccurate information can be disseminated. We return to the issue of fake news in the Afterword.

(76) Stuff that shows prejudice. I don't like racism or sexism. I didn't say anything. Stuff that I will respond to includes a lot of pseudo-science new age stuff. It doesn't offend me so much as annoy me it people don't verify facts. [Q26-22]

The online space is often contrasted with face-to-face communication, which is seen as better suited to serious conversation. This comparison suggests a wider media ideology in which different forms of mediation (including face-to-face interactions) are seen as fulfilling different but complementary objectives, suggesting that one platform can only be understood in relation to other possibilities. Such a comparison is made by the following respondent as they explain what they get 'bothered' about:

(77) Usually about American politics, conceal and carry laws or abortion restrictions. I might get bothered by it, but I don't post about it. I would prefer to have those conversations face-to-face. [Q26-12]

As the following respondent suggests and as also discussed in the previous chapter, one needs to exercise more care on Facebook because it relies almost solely on the written medium, and thus excludes paralinguistic cues.

(78) I try to be careful not to offend anyone and so I don't post about politics or religion. ... For some reason, social networks seem to amplify the effects of someone's opinions. Perhaps because you can focus solely on their literal words with no sub-communication that you would have in real life. [Q24-55]

So far in the analysis presented above, it is evident that instances in which people were offended did not lead to confrontation or debate, but rather to a more discreet avoidance of the offending situation, either by unfriending, blocking or doing nothing. This may be due to the perception of Facebook as not being an appropriate place for debate and also that, as a communicative space, Facebook is meant to be for lighthearted trivial content, rather than discussion of more serious topics. As such, users do not see the need to respond to views they deem offensive and instead work to maintain convivial relations on the site.

Negotiation of Offence

Only in a few cases did some form of negotiation around an offending post take place. These cases are important both for highlighting the infrequency of such interactions and for showing that effective negotiation of this kind—and a consequent reconsideration of people's positions—is possible on Facebook, despite suggestions to the contrary voiced by other respondents. We saw earlier how one respondent asked a Friend to untag him in a photo after having to explain to 'several people' that it was not a picture of his girlfriend. Another example of negotiation is as follows.

(79) A cousin publicly posted a meme-style pic of Jesus casually throwing the word "fuckin'" into a public statement. I commented telling her I'd unfriend her if she was going to keep doing that kind of thing. She got really upset that I'd commented that way on her wall. I deleted my comment, apologized, and thought a lot more about what should be said and done in private and what in public. [Q26-28]

Interestingly, in the above examples, the negotiation led to an action on Facebook being undone—a photo untagged and a comment deleted, respectively. In these cases, people's modified understandings of an interaction, as co-constructed through their negotiations, produce a form of context design in which an earlier state—an earlier version of Facebook—is reinstated. This also happened in a more controversial way when the administrator of a group that our interviewee Heather belongs to deleted one of her comments. In this case, it is clear that an earlier state could not be returned to and that the act of deleting someone else's post itself fulfils a communicative function, that of flagging the comment up as a problem: 'because him deleting the comment is saying 'this is an issue' … people are like 'oh what was missing and everyone is talking about what was deleted'. This imagined scenario leads Heather to feel 'like "oh no, I screwed up there"' with potential implications for her future behaviour online. The administrator's potentially provocative act, however, was a very rare one in a dataset that otherwise highlighted the non-confrontational ways in which our respondents dealt with, or avoided, acts of offence on Facebook.

Offline Text Trajectories and Face-to-Face Negotiations

Finally, it was evident, particularly from comments made in the interviews, that instances of offence that occurred on Facebook had ramifications that extended beyond the online space into people's offline interactions, where they can be negotiated further: Jacob reported, for example that his offended wife raised the issue of his failure to Like the post about their baby not on Facebook but 'at the dinner table', although it appears that the matter is never fully resolved. For Heather, on the other hand, the issue is that an online offence cannot always travel easily or smoothly into a face-to-face situation. The fact that 'no discussion ever came out' of her deleted comment is awkward:

(80) I had never actually had a face to face argument with her [the girl she had potentially offended in the deleted comment] but it always felt like there was unsaid tension between us. [Heather, interview]

In the case of the offence caused by Heather's post about foxes, there is again 'this awkward tension' when Heather meets in person one of the women she offended and, as described earlier, struggles to find a way to raise the incident: 'It was like "how do you bring that up?" "Hi Anna, listen, about the fox thing …"'. Recontextualised into the physical space, their emotive online confrontation becomes something that cannot easily be mentioned, and in this way affects their offline relationship.

In the following comment made in interview, Jessica also appears cognisant of the uneasy relation between the online and offline. Her awareness that the trajectory of a post is not necessarily restricted to Facebook is evident when she describes how she sometimes meets up with other members of a Facebook group in an offline situation and they talk about Facebook posts. She suggests that although people might think the act of posting is 'done', their posts are being given new life in these 'circles of gossip'. The problem, as she explains, is that:

(81) These people are posting with the idea that they have posted it and it is done but it is not, it is being taken offline and being talked about in person again, and it is being rehashed in their memory ... I am forming this idea about them, this personality, even though I may potentially never meet them and if I do then I am going on things like 'oh right, you posted about that topic and I didn't really like you' or 'I really want to look at your profile because that really cracks me up and you never change it' so yes ... You get these weird identity creations of people that are probably unfair and untrue. [Jessica, interview]

Here, the problem as Jessica sees it is that people are often unaware of the future offline trajectories of their posts, and how these posts can be transformed through offline gossip. The interviews therefore highlighted the intermingling between the offline and the online, and the potential implications of online offences for offline conviviality and relationships, whilst at the same time suggesting that the offline recontextualisation of online posts can generate very different interpretations and patterns of interaction than they did online.

Actions to Avoid Offending Others

Tolerating Difference

Evident across the ways in which our participants claimed to respond to being offended is the suggestion that acts that cause offence are to some extent to be expected and tolerated on a site like Facebook, given the potential ambiguity of the written medium, the difficulty of extended discussion, and the intradiverse nature of the audience. Although a factor in explaining incidents when participants were offended, this tolerance was more marked in their explanations as to how they might have offended others. In explaining what s/he would not post, for example, the respondent below wrote:

(82) negative comments about anybody who might my posts; don't want them to see what I'm thinking. any opinions that might be controversial (politics, etc.); don't want to receive negative

attention, and since I have such a wide range of Facebook friends, it doesn't seem unlikely that somebody could take issue with what i post. [Q17-51]

Meanwhile, another reflected that: 'I don't hold grudges and soon forget most of the rubbish I type on Facebook' [Q22-42].

As well as highlighting people's awareness of their intradiverse audience, this tolerance also suggests that, through avoiding potential conflict or 'negative attention', our participants are to some extent sidestepping the need to engage in any depth with more weighty or contentious debate.

Avoidance Tactics

Strategies that people use for pre-emptively taking actions to avoid situations where they may cause offence and in turn provoke responses which they themselves will find offensive, speak very directly to the way in which they are actively designing the context for their communication, either by avoidance strategies, or by using the affordances of the site to limit what can be seen by whom. As the person below comments, an awareness of the (semi-) public nature of the space prompts a certain circumspection about what is posted and how:

(83) I understand that anything posted is broadcasted for the world to see, so everything that goes up there first goes through a round of filter that I create for myself. [Q24-56]

The next example likewise talks of a process of 'customising' posts, based on a projection of how s/he thinks they are likely to be received by sections of the intradiverse network of which s/he is a part. In this example, two particular factions in his/her network thus have a regulative influence: 'arguments with other church members' and his or her mother's distress. These scenarios are likely based on his/her previous experience of the site—for example on earlier instances where his/her mother was upset by her posts—thus we see how past experience with a technology feeds into context design processes.

(84) I am part of a very conservative religious group but hold very progressive views. I heavily customize my posts in order to not get into arguments with other church members about my

'unorthodox' views. I also try to avoid posting a lot of negative news articles about the country I am now a permanent resident of (Korea) because it makes my mother upset to read those articles. [Q24-21]

The following respondent is also reflective of the way posts may be read by others, and how this has resulted in him/her rinsing the feed, as their awareness of how early posts might be interpreted by an audience grew.

(85) I have become more selfconscious about what I am posting and who's reading it which has made me post less than when I first opened my account in 2008. In fact, I went through and deleted most of my postings that I didn't deem neutral should I add new people and they mine / stalk through my account. I use the word stalk purposefully as it seems like if you go back a few years and comment on old pictures, it feels like a strange invasion of privacy because you / that person wasn't there at the moment. Silly for something that is public / semi-public / allowing others to see. [Q14-42]

In these examples, we see how people respond to previous experiences on the site in order to maintain convivial relations with Facebook Friends.

Hiding Posts to Avoid Controversy

As well as pre-emptive avoidance, another strategy is the deletion of individual posts that show up on their wall. As these are directed specifically at the individual's wall, they become part of the visible profile that is projected by that wall, and a product therefore of the way an individual's identity is composed of the beliefs others have about them as these are reflected in affiliations they make for the individual (i.e. the types of posts they think will be of interest to the individual). When elements of this identity differ from the one that the individual is trying to curate for themselves, they can in response either engage with the post, or delete it. In the following example the poster has a difference of opinion with her husband about the type of profile she is happy to present in this forum, and for this reason removes things he posts to her wall:

(86) I'm extremely, probably overly, concerned about this. My social media image is very non-confrontational. Very bubble gum sweet. My husband will post things on my page that I delete or hide. For example, he links to a story about a Canadian lady who stopped on the highway for an animal and two people were killed when they ran into her vehicle. He called the lady a psycho. I hid the post, but people commented and I had to respond feeling sympathy for the whole situation. Now I just delete anything that's slightly controversial. [Q24-3]

We also saw deletion being used as a tactic by the moderator of Heather's group, and it was also raised as a possibility by the respondent who moderated a parents' forum.

Regulating Style and Content as a Form of Context Design

A more subtle tactic engaged in by some of the respondents in response to their intradiverse networks was to take care over the way they composed their posts in terms of style and register. In the following response, despite aiming at a particular group of friends (thus creating a particular space by addressing an imagined audience), the poster nevertheless takes care over the presentation of what is written because of their awareness of the wider potential audience.

(87) My typical status update is about an important event or something happened during the day that really surprised me and I would like to share with my friends on Facebook. Mostly they are about political events and news. Sometimes I also like to share some thoughts about the previous night with some of the people I was hanging out with. Both of these types of status update are usually aimed at specific friends that might be concerned about what I'm writing (I usually tag the in the status update). My writing style in not too formal, but never impolite. Possibly with a good linguistic register, often higher than the normally spoken one. I usually tend to recheck what I wrote in order to avoid typos. This is because I always keep in mind that Facebook is a public place, and I like it to be so. [Q14-140]

In interview, Jessica similarly explained how the styling of posts was to her a strategy for dealing with her large varied audience, and specifically for restricting her interactions on the site: 'I am purposely wording what I do put on-line to be more specific so that I can try and limit some of the people that I don't want to interact with'. From the other side of this context design process, Heather talked about not being offended by someone whose opinions she disagreed with because he wrote in a measured way: 'this guy was a bit more measured and he didn't offend me in that conversation. I didn't agree with his position in the end but he didn't offend me'. Her remarks suggest that the adoption of particular styles and registers may be effective in reducing offence.

Although not a frequently mentioned tactic in our survey data, the use of linguistic or social strategies such as these have been documented in studies of interactional data (Seargeant et al. 2012). According to Marwick and boyd (2014), Facebook users can 'hide in plain sight' by posting vague, contextual posts or oblique cultural references in a process they call 'social steganography'. It is possible—although not verifiable with our data—that more of our respondents may have engaged also in such practices, but that these strategies may be deployed below their level of conscious reflection. Whilst in some respects an indication of the limitations of our methodology, this observation also usefully raises questions regarding the extent to which context design itself always operates above the level of consciousness. Such questions, unfortunately, are beyond the scope of this book, which focuses on the extent to which media and language ideologies, and their impact on communicative strategies, can be articulated by users.

Moderating One's Behaviour to Having Offended

Despite the relaxed approach to dealing with incidents and the general tolerance towards being offended that is suggested across the survey data, a number of respondents noted that they had changed their behaviour as a response to acts of offence on Facebook. Usually, such incidents had made them more cautious and careful, they avoided politics as a topic, they posted less, and they paid more attention to how they wrote—for example by avoiding 'rants'.

(88) I see how posts that weren't directly aimed at me have offended me. As such, I scrutinize my posts. My primary aim in posting is instigating smiles and laughter amongst my friends. [Q30-5]

(89)   I'm careful anyway, but yeah people getting upset has made me more cautious. [Q30-10]

(90)   I'm more aware of how a simple rant could offend someone, and keep rants to facebook groups where I know how they will be received, as opposed to on my own wall. [Q30-11]

(91)   I write a little less about toilet humor by request. (Ironically, I've had people complain that I post less about toilet humor) [Q30-42]

The ways in which participants claimed to have responded to their having offended others offers clear examples of how context design operates on the site. The last post above, although clearly written in jest, illustrates quite effectively the feeling that on Facebook you cannot please everyone, and it can be read as a comment on the fact that adjusting one's behaviour to avoid offending is likely to be an on-going, complex process of negotiation.

We saw earlier how Jessica manipulated her settings so as to avoid being alerted to comments on her posts. A similar example of this aspect of context design emerged from the other interviews. Jacob is aware that he does not set his privacy setting very high, and in fact explains that he keeps his Facebook feed public so that he does not start treating it as private:

(92)   most of the things that end up on my page I mostly keep that public intentionally so that anybody can view it whether they have signed up to Facebook or not. I do that intentionally just because it helps me kind of see it more for what it is ... I think what it does, it essentially forces me not to put anything too private on Facebook to begin with. [Jacob, interview]

By keeping his privacy settings low so as to encourage him to treat the site as public, Jacob exploits the affordances of Facebook (its more public settings) in order to shape the way he designs the contexts for his posts. This act of context design is driven by his belief that the privacy settings are not effective and by his ideas about the likelihood of data leakage on Facebook, of the unpredictable trajectories of posts, and ultimately then the fear of entextualisation which could result. As he put it:

(93) If I put something up there and I select it only to be for this group of friends or whatever it is really not, like anybody can copy it, take a screen shoot, it goes public, it has the potential to go to a public domain. [Jacob, interview]

In other words, his media ideologies as they relate to Facebook and the question of privacy, as well as his awareness of affordances such as the privacy settings and of the possible future trajectories of his posts, all determine what and how he designs the context for his posts.

Summary

In relation to acts of offence on Facebook, conviviality involves ignoring views which offend individuals and accepting that a certain amount of offence is inevitable (*tolerating difference*); blocking people or posts who have offended or been offended (*avoiding difference*); and, in a few cases, moderating one's behaviour in response to having offended (*reducing difference*). These responses, while not universal, may be encouraged by various features of the communicative situation. First, the communicative norms that have emerged from Facebook networks include those that state that interactions should be affirmative and light-hearted (McLaughlin and Vitak 2011), and certain of our participants referred to their perception that Facebook was not 'the place for deep or meaningful debate, it's for pictures of funny things and looking at people when bored'; in line with this, the presentation of a positive persona appears also to be a communicative principle on the site. As Chun and Walters (2011) note of YouTube, the structural affordances do not necessarily encourage debate—in relation to Facebook, for example there is currently a variety of 'Like' options but not an explicit 'Disagree' option—and this again was an opinion voiced by a number of our respondents. Notwithstanding this, it is likely that social network sites such as Facebook encourage reflexivity, not only because of the written medium but also the incentive to respond to others' posts in various ways, be it by Liking, commenting, sharing and so forth (Androutsopoulos and Staehr 2017). Taking this into account, the annoyances and frustrations that participants in our study report feeling suggest that people are to some extent reflecting on others' posts, and engaging either intellectually or emotionally with them, but that they often simply choose not to respond to them in a public way or in a confrontational manner.

Second, the participant structure of Facebook seems often to militate against argument and strongly-expressed disagreement, with responses from the survey recognising the intradiverse ego-centred nature of their network and commenting on the way they 'cannot defriend' various connections for social reasons. People appear constrained not only by their strong ties and a desire not to upset parents, partners or close friends, but also by their awareness of the acquaintances or weak ties at the periphery of their network and the possibility of their behaviour being evaluated by those whose values they are less sure about. This aspect of intradiversity appears to create a situation in which people are thus constraining themselves in front of strangers, whilst also being aware in a more specific way which posts may upset or offend their intimates.

DESIGNING THE IDEA OF FACEBOOK

The implication of online conviviality, based on our data, is twofold therefore: on the one hand, it suggests that, as in the case of superdiverse urban communities, people engage in civil behaviour on Facebook as a means of getting along and getting things done (which in this case might involve curating a particular profile and maintaining relationships). On the other hand it also suggests that, for these Facebook users at least, their interactions on the site are not enabling them to engage with other viewpoints or to change their own worldviews in any significant manner. We have seen how people respond to opposing viewpoints not by engaging the individual in debate, or challenging those views, but more often by blocking their posts or unfriending them. Similarly, we have seen how people have very definite and specific ideas about what appropriate behaviour on Facebook involves, and that they use these ideas as a basis for blocking people whose actions differ from this.

This leads us on to the concept of context design as the way in which newsfeeds are managed at a micro-interactional level. Our starting assumption is that a user's experience of a social media site is determined in part by their ideas about it and how these ideas shape their subsequent behaviour; that is, how their beliefs about how Facebook should be used (and a myriad of other factors) feed into their context design processes. This was recognised by one of our interviewees, Jacob, who said:

(94) I think that the topics that are chosen actually end up shaping what Facebook is for many people so I think in certain groups of people choosing to talk about different topics that becomes their Facebook experience I think.... Facebook can be so many things to so many people. [Jacob, interview]

Our argument is that Facebook users take into account a particularly complex set of factors when designing a post, including feedback from an often highly intradiverse audience (defined in terms of demographics, values and beliefs, and by their differing relationships with the node user), their media ideologies as they relate to Facebook and their understanding of the affordances of the site, their purposes and the norms of communication, and, importantly, the desire to performatively co-construct a particular kind of social identity. Also shaping what they post and how is recognition of the likely yet unpredictable trajectory their posts may take. In discussing context design in this book, it is worth reiterating that we are foregrounding the communicative actions of the user (as these are reflectively expressed in our data), and not focusing directly on the influence of features such as the personalisation algorithm which the newsfeed uses to rank the relevance of information that it displays, and which also has an effect on the unique context that is created by and for each individual user (for discussion of the interface between user context design and algorithmic personalisation see Seargeant and Tagg forthcoming). However, as we discuss in the Afterword, the arguments made in this book point to the need to take into account how users' awareness of affordances and their implications and their underlying media ideologies might determine the way they behave in a space also shaped in part by algorithms and other company design decisions.

In relation to context design, our elicited data has suggested that Facebook users are aware of various aspects of intradiversity—including the different values held by different Friends, the different identity groups they align with, and the implications of the different relationships they have with each one—and that this awareness shapes how they design the context for their postings. By revealing conviviality to be an important principle on Facebook, we also showed how the desire to maintain civil relations, as well as to project a positive and likeable persona, were also likely to shape people's actions and intentions for the site. Context design was shown to be a reactive process, by which people responded to what they liked and disliked about behaviour on the site and sought to frame their own posts in ways which downplayed certain aspects of the site and promoted others. Thus people's responses to earlier behaviour that they considered offensive fed into their future processes of context design. Given the overwhelming agreement that the main cause of offence was opinions with which individuals disagreed, people claimed both to avoid making political or otherwise controversial statements and to ignore (or at least not engage with) political views which appeared on their newsfeed. The perception, however, that Facebook is not a place for political debate and is instead suited for the trivial and light-hearted clearly contrasts with how the site is often being used and thus points to a contradiction between how Facebook is perceived and the actual role it plays in society. Context design, then, is a process which can rest on multiple, often conflicting, media and language ideologies, but which shapes the way the site is both perceived and viewed as a communicative space.

CHAPTER 7

Afterword: Beyond Facebook

Abstract The book concludes with an Afterword considering how the findings emerging from *Creating Facebook* relate to the wider ecosystem of different forms of social media (e.g. Twitter, YouTube, Snapchat), which provide different affordances and on which different patterns of social engagement have developed. It then reflects on the wider significance of our research project for contemporary social relations and political stance-taking on Facebook.

Keywords Affordances · Critical digital literacy · Filter bubble Mediascape · Platforms

What Doughnuts Tell Us About Platforms and Media Ideologies

In this chapter, we explore the wider implications of *Creating Facebook* for our understanding of social media communication, contemporary social relations and political stance-taking.

In early 2010, a meme was widely circulated which offered a simple, tongue-in-cheek explanation of the difference between the main social media sites, with reference to the topic of doughnuts. It reduced each site to the type of behaviour it is most typically used for (or perceived to be used for), as captured in a single-sentence post about the user's relationship to doughnuts:

© The Author(s) 2017
C. Tagg et al., *Taking Offence on Social Media*,
DOI 10.1007/978-3-319-56717-4_7

Facebook—I like doughnuts

Twitter—I'm eating a #doughnut

Blogger—Read about my doughnut eating experiences

Foursquare—This is where I eat doughnuts

YouTube—Watch me eating a doughnut

LinkedIn—My skills include doughnut eating

Pinterest—Here's a doughnut recipe

LastFM—Now listening to "doughnuts"

Instagram—Here's a vintage photo of my doughnut

Google+—I'm a Google employee who eats doughnuts

The use of doughnuts as the recurring topic for each post indexes the sort of triviality that is often associated with the content of online communication, on which we have commented earlier in the book, whilst the first-person perspective is suggestive of the self-centred nature of this communication. (As an aside, it is also notable that some of these particular sites are already dated—and have been replaced in popularity by others—only 3 or 4 years after the meme was current.)

What is being highlighted, however, is what users see as the primary function to which each of these sites is put. In other words, the sites are defined by how people *use* them; this becomes their identity, such that it can be parodied in a single proposition. The way each site is used is in part a product of the affordances intended by the site designers and exploited by users (e.g. Instagram was designed to be primarily for the sharing of photos and, at least in the first few years of its existence, the use of filters to produce a 'vintage' look was one of its attractions). But site identities are also tied to the media ideologies that are associated with each site. The user actions which define each platform's distinct identity produce and reproduce the attitudes people have towards the sites, and how they interpret their specific use-value within the wider ecology of social media. In other words, the distinct site identities are constructed by what people think and do with them, and how they frame their communication based on these beliefs and experiences.

If we look more closely at the main platforms in use in the early decades of the twenty-first century, we can begin to flesh out how users' ideologies—their ideas about what the site is for and how it should be used—contribute to the particular character associated with each site, and from this perspective, consider how our findings from Facebook relate to the wider ecosystem of different forms of social media, all of which provide a slightly different range of affordances and thus different patterns of social engagement. It is of note, however, that at present there is markedly less work examining these types of interaction on other platforms, and thus the extent to which our findings have more general applicability is an area which would benefit from future study. Nor is there much work (as yet) which explores how users move between these different social media platforms in their everyday online interactions (but see Adami 2014).

In contrast to the Facebook interactions discussed in this book, the image messaging application Snapchat appears to be encouraging users to bond rather than gain social capital, supporting more intimate and close relationships (Piwek and Joinson 2015) than many of those described by our respondents. Snapchat seems to be used (at this moment in time) not as a sharing platform but as a means of connecting with trusted ties (Bayer et al. 2015). A similar appraisal has been made for WhatsApp (Takahashi 2014), which is seen as offering a safe space where people can express themselves and which seems to encourage more conversational exchanges than earlier messaging systems, such as SMS for which people were more likely to be paying per message (Evans and Tagg 2016). Skype too emerges from the literature as offering individuals a more intimate experience than they have with other forms of social media (Miller and Sinanan 2014), perhaps because it affords the possibility of interactants seeing each other in potentially private spaces. The ways in which these platforms are currently being used thus differs primarily from the uses our participants made of Facebook in terms of their smaller, less diverse and more intimate audiences. This is likely to render conviviality—which has been found to characterise diverse public or parochial places, rather than private ones—less relevant in shaping communicative dynamics; that is, the difference may be less of an issue and participants more likely to engage deeply with each other's concerns and viewpoints. In terms of context design, it is likely that participants in intimate exchanges will be able to draw more confidently on an assumed shared background.

As we saw in Chap. 3, users of YouTube seem to operate at the other end of the spectrum. Moor et al. (2010), for example, note that people perceive a great deal of flaming on YouTube, possibly to do with the fact that it is an arena where people comment without knowing each other. They suggest that unintended acts of aggression might be misinterpreted in some instances, with people reacting to perceived flames with further flames. There is also some suggestion that flaming is taken as a norm of the site (Moor et al. 2010), which may go some way to explain the way in which aggression so easily escalates. Although there is, perhaps surprisingly, not a great deal of scholarship on the taking of offence on Twitter, Page (2014b) notes that people not responding to complaints leads to further offence (suggesting a similar escalation, as noted for YouTube), and there are clearly high profile cases on Twitter which are reminiscent of what happens on YouTube (see our overview in Chap. 3). As well as leading to acts of aggression, the non-reciprocal model means Twitter is associated more with the production of social capital than bonding (Hofer and Aubert 2013), and in this way contrasts with platforms associated with greater intimacy.

To the extent that Twitter users are less likely to have existing relationships with their online interactants than we saw among our Facebook users, conviviality may be less of a guiding principle than on Facebook (and the same may be argued in relation to much interaction on YouTube). Although people may try to avoid conflict on Twitter, there may be less need to achieve conviviality in order to maintain and bolster the array of complex offline relationships our participants discussed in relation to Facebook. This is not to say that processes of context design are any less complex for those who engage in public interactions on a site like Twitter or YouTube, but rather that they are likely to be realised differently. Whilst context design for our Facebook users involved the careful management of various offline relationships, the audience for a public site is at once much larger and more indeterminate: 'it is everyone who has or will have access to the Internet' (Wesch 2009, p. 22).

Interestingly, young people seem to worry less about privacy on Twitter than on Facebook, possibly because they use it for different types of content (Jeong and Coyle 2014). As Miller (2016) documents in his ethnography of an English village, some teenagers appear to be using the site in ways that differ strikingly from adults, and describe the site as private and intimate. One could therefore hypothesise that although for people commenting on Justin Bieber tweets, their experience of Twitter may be more like that of YouTube users, the potential for offence between people with reciprocal relationships might be more similar to Facebook. The different ways in which a site like Twitter (and others) are used cautions against the tendency to assume that online behaviour is determined by a site's affordances, and points again to the role that user decision-making, purpose and awareness plays in the identity that a site comes to have. For example, Instagram, about which there is presently very little scholarship, appears to support a similar type of interaction as Twitter, but research suggests that people find Instagram 'nicer' than Twitter (Miller 2016); why this is so will have emerged in complex ways for certain communities or networks from the interplay between available functionalities and user ideology and agency.

The kind of interaction hosted by different sites, then, must be seen as both contextualised and emergent (and therefore only ever a snapshot in time), dependent on the different ways in which affordances are taken up by different individuals and groups, the ways that users come to associate particular patterns of interaction with particular sites, and how their behaviour goes on to shape future design decisions and subsequent user behaviour.

FACEBOOK, CONVIVIALITY AND THE FILTER BUBBLE

The findings from *Creating Facebook*, therefore, need to be understood against the background of the wider mediascape in which social media users operate and which likely shapes their ideas and attitudes towards Facebook, as well as their understanding of the particular affordances and communicative dynamic that has become associated with this particular site.

To summarise our research, the social media users we surveyed and interviewed in this project were overwhelmingly most likely to be offended on Facebook by political, religious, sexist or racist opinions with which they disagreed. In the main, they accepted that some disagreement was inevitable, thus showing a certain awareness of the participant structure of Facebook and the likelihood of *intradiversity*, and many people simply ignored the offending posts. Where they did respond, they generally did so non-aggressively by ensuring through various methods that they no longer had access to such posts. Their responses suggest that these Facebook users are interested neither in argument (of the kind described on sites like YouTube) nor, for the most part, in more reasoned debate around differing views. Rather, we have a very different outcome: on the one hand, the removal of posts and Friends suggests an attempt to construct a newsfeed filled only or predominantly with opinions with which they agree, a phenomenon that Jones and Hafner (2012, p. 126) call the 'ghetto-ization' of the internet and which we see as arising in part out of processes of context design; on the other, we see a tolerance of difference that is paradoxically indifferent: people will endure opposing views but they do not challenge or engage with them.

As a general trend, the research thus revealed *conviviality* to be an overarching principle for this particular type of 'ego-centred' social media encounter, and this has important implications for our understanding of contemporary social relations. In short, if users' attitudes towards difference stop short of any deep engagement with opposing political views or social practices, then Facebook is unlikely to encourage mutual engagement and understanding across cultural, political and social boundaries in a way imagined in the early days of the internet. In line with our conclusion that conviviality is a principle guiding context design on Facebook, it is perhaps not surprising that one of the findings from this research is that Facebook as a communicative space is best suited, in the opinion of many of our respondents, to topics which are positive, light-hearted and 'fun'. As evident in our data analysis, there is also a strong trend in the survey and interview responses suggesting that Facebook is not suited for topics which involve debate, especially around politics or anything which may provoke controversy. The rationale for such an ideology is not something that the research investigated directly—we had no questions explicitly asking after this—but a reason that was often volunteered by the participants was that the affordances of online interaction do not lend themselves well to reasoned debate, and that misunderstandings can easily occur due to the lack of paralinguistic contextualising cues and the sort of dialogic negotiation that face-to-face interaction can accommodate. This view of the relative merits of face-to-face versus online communication for smooth communication appears to be an entrenched belief which is found both in the reflective responses of our participants, but also in the literature on the propensity of online interaction for aggression and antipathy (see Chap. 3).

Importantly, however, there is a paradox in the fact that participants in this project are arguing that Facebook should be a place for more trivial or light-hearted content on the back of their complaints about how currently it is *not* constituted as such. Despite people reporting that they do not see Facebook as a suitable place for discussion of serious or contentious issues, our research also indicates that a great deal of people do use it for expressing political views. This may be an issue of what counts, to them, as a political view, and it is only the more extreme and potentially contentious issues they avoid. It was also notable that answers to questions about causing offence themselves picked up on issues that we would deem more trivial than those about being offended, which again is likely to do with perception, as well as strategies of self-presentation. Nonetheless, the ideologies that feed people's context design strategies, and which shape the space as one in which conviviality is a determining principle and the trivial is preferred to the serious or contentious, are reactive to ways in which, at present, it is used to express political opinions.

An important—and consequential—issue in this respect is that whilst the overwhelming trend in people's expressed opinions is that Facebook is *not* suited to debate and disagreement, and that things should be kept light trivial, this runs counter to the way that Facebook is emerging as a very important news media site: 'it's no longer just a technology company, but a media company—*the* media company', as Solon (2016) writes, and one which, for over two-fifths of the American adult population, now acts as a primary source of news (Gottfried and Shearer 2016). As such, it operates as a place where political perspectives and opinions are consumed and shared, and where people's beliefs are validated. Rather than simply being a forum for entertainment it appears, therefore, to have a serious political influence (Isaac 2016). In this context, the strategies that people have revealed in this research—the fact that they avoid conflict and engagement when faced with values they disagree with, and that they design the space in ways which allow for conviviality—contribute to the way in which 'filter bubbles' are created and maintained. These create an 'epistemic closure', as Benton (2016) terms it, which comes from only being exposed to views and perspectives that you agree with. What we are calling conviviality contributes to processes of confirmation bias, and appears to produce—or at least contribute to—a polarising of world views rather than the opportunity for dialogue across ideological lines.

Much of the media discussion around the reasons for the phenomenon of filter bubbles has focused on the structure and affordances of the site itself—how Facebook's algorithm, designed as it is for creating a positive user experience, aims to feed people what they want—and there have been calls in the media for Facebook itself to act to address these issues (Isaac 2016; Solon 2016). The affordances of the site, as these are influenced by the algorithm and are designed by the site's architects, are certainly an important element in this, but what this research illustrates is that of equal importance is what people do with the site and how they fashion the experience of it as a communicative space through *context design* processes. Although not a main focus of our research at the time, an awareness that the technology behind Facebook may not be neutral was evident in our data, particularly in the interviews. Jacob, for example, suggests that coming across offensive or unwanted content on Facebook is unlikely because of Facebook's algorithms:

(95)   I think there is something that I don't want to see, don't want to read, I just skip over it, I just choose not to see it. It is pretty much as simple as that and I think now a days that the algorithms are so that they know what you want to see. [Jacob, interview]

Partly as a result of this and other ideas he has about Facebook, Jacob does not feel he has much control about the future trajectories of his posts or how they will be interpreted, but at the same time he is fairly relaxed about the possibility of offending or being offended. Similarly, Jessica also shows her awareness of the Facebook platform as playing a role in shaping experiences on the site and determining how posts might be entextualised:

(96)   What others are forgetting is that there is still somebody behind the wall, think 'Wizard of Oz' who are running the machine so somebody is seeing it somewhere and you can assume that you don't have total privacy. [Jessica, interview]

In contrast to Jacob, however, Jessica both uses the site as a way of raising important topics and making her points of view known and, as detailed throughout this book, engages in processes of elaborate and careful consideration regarding what she posts, how, and what the implications may be. Unlike Jacob, who keeps his profile public in order for this to act as a constraint on his behaviour, she keeps her account private, and in fact, keeps her groups separate from her personal profile. As these examples suggest, what is important is not the technology per se—although this will undoubtedly be shaping both Jessica's and Jacob's newsfeeds—but the different ways in which they respond to their understanding of the algorithms and affordances behind Facebook. In other words, they are not victims to the technological determinism of the algorithmic environment in which they operate, but, due to their digital literacy awareness, have a certain amount of agency in how they design their experience of communication on the site.

Responses from across our data suggest that, for many of our participants at least, online context design is a semi-conscious and self-reflexive process, and there is evidence in some cases of quite a sophisticated awareness of the intradiverse nature of Facebook networks as well as a sense of agency and confidence in how online audiences can be managed. We would, therefore, argue that it is the intersection between affordances and user perception, between algorithms and personal choices that determine how the site is used and experienced. People's awareness of the site's functionalities, and their perceptions of their own agency in exploiting them for their own social purposes, is built up from their experience in using the site, which is in turn shaped by the extent and nature of their awareness. What this means is that navigating this complex communicative space is a learnt practice. One potential consequence of this is that online users need a critical understanding of the implications of the algorithms and company decisions that underlie their interactions, so that they are able to take these into account when predicting the likely trajectory of their posts and managing the content of their newsfeeds. In this, an understanding of the context in which online communication takes place, and the way this context is shaped by those involved, is a vital part of successful social interaction in the twenty-first century.

Bibliography

Adami, E. 2014. Retwitting, reposting, repinning; reshaping identities online: Towards a social semiotic multimodal of digital remediation. *Lingue e Letterature d'Oriente e d'Occidente* 3: 223–243.

Androutsopoulos, J. 2014a. Languaging when contexts collapse: Audience design in social networking. *Discourse, Context and Media* 4–5: 62–73.

Androutsopoulos, J. 2014b. Moments of sharing: Entextualisation and linguistic repertoires in social networking. *Journal of Pragmatics* 73: 4–18.

Androutsopoulos, J. 2015. Networked multilingualism: Some language practices on Facebook and their implications. *International Journal of Bilingualism* 19 (2): 185–205.

Androutsopoulos, J., and K. Juffermans. 2014. Digital language practices in superdiversity: Introduction. *Discourse, Context & Media* 4–5: 1–6.

Androutsopoulos, J., and A. Staehr. 2017. Moving methods online: Researching digital language practices. In *The Routledge handbook of language and superdiversity*, ed. A. Creese and A. Blackledge. Abingdon: Routledge.

Angouri, J., and T. Tseliga. 2010. You have no idea what you are talking about! From e-disagreement to e-impoliteness in two online fora. *Journal of Politeness Research* 6: 57–82.

Barbera, P.J.T., J. Jost, J.A. Tucker Nagler, and R. Bonneau. 2015. Tweeting from left to right: Is online political communication more than an echo chamber? *Psychological Science* 26 (10): 1531–1542.

Baron, N. 2007. My best day: Presentation of self and social manipulation in Facebook and IM. Paper presented at Internet Research 8.0 Association of Internet Researchers, Oct 17–20, Vancouver.

Barton, D., and C. Lee. 2013. *Language online: Investigating digital texts and practices.* New York: Routledge.

Bauman, R. 1992. Contextualization, tradition, and the dialogue of genres: Icelandic legends of the *kraftaskáld*. In *Rethinking context: Language as an interactive phenomenon*, ed. A. Duranti and C. Goodwin, 125–146. Cambridge: Cambridge University Press.

Bauman, R., and C.L. Briggs. 1990. Poetics and performance as critical perspectives on social life. *Annual Review of Anthropology* 19: 59–88.

Bayer, J.B., N.B. Ellison, S.Y. Schoenebeck, and E.B. Falk. 2015. Sharing the small moments: Ephemeral social interaction on Snapchat. *Information, Communication and Society* 19 (7): 956–977.

Baym, N. 2010. *Personal connections in the digital age*. Cambridge: Polity Press.

Bell, A. 1984. Language style as audience design. *Language in Society* 13 (2): 145–204.

Bell, A. 1999. Styling the other to design the self: a study in New Zealand identity making. *Journal of Sociolinguistics* 3 (4): 523–541.

Bell, A. 2001. Back in style: Reworking audience design. In *Style and Sociolinguistic Variation*, ed. P. Eckert and J. R. Rickford, 139–169. Cambridge: Cambridge University Press.

Benton, J. 2016. The forces that drove this election's media failure are likely to get worse. *Nieman Journalism Lab*, November 9. Available at https://www.niemanlab.org/2016/11/the-forces-that-drove-this-elections-media-failure-are-likely-to-get-worse/.

Bixby, S. 2016. The end of Trump: How Facebook deepens millennials' confirmation bias. *The Guardian*, October 1. https://www.theguardian.com/us-news/2016/oct/01/millennials-facebook-politics-bias-social-media.

Blommaert, J. 2005. *Discourse: A critical introduction*. Cambridge: Cambridge University Press.

Blommaert, J. 2010. *The Sociolinguistics of Globalisation*. Cambridge: Cambridge University Press.

Blommaert, J., and P. Varis. 2013. Enough is enough: The heretics of authenticity in superdiversity. In *Linguistic superdiversity in urban areas: Research approaches*, ed. J. Duarte and I. Gogolin, 143–159. Amsterdam: John Benjamins.

Bolter, J.D., and R. Grusin. 1999. *Remediation: Understanding new media*. Cambridge, MA: The MIT Press.

Bou-Franch, P., and P. Garcés-Conejos Blitvich. 2014. Conflict management in massive polylogues: A case study from YouTube. *Journal of Pragmatics* 73: 19–36.

boyd, d. 2001. *Taken out of context: American teen sociality in networked publics*. Unpublished doctoral dissertation, University of California, Berkeley.

boyd, d. 2008. Facebook's privacy trainwreck: Exposure, invasion and social convergence. *The International Journal of Research into New Media Technologies* 14 (1): 13–20.

boyd, d. 2012. Networked privacy. *Surveillance and Society* 10 (3–4): 348–350.
boyd, d. 2014. *It's complicated: The social lives of networked teens.* New Haven, NJ: Yale University Press.
boyd, d., and A. Marwick. 2011. Social privacy in networked publics: Teens' attitudes, practices, and strategies. In *Proceedings of the "A Decade in Internet Time: A Symposium on the Dynamics of the Internet and Society"*, 1–29, Sept. 21–24, University of Oxford.
Broadbent, S., and V. Bauwens. 2008. Understanding convergence. *Interactions* 15 (1): 29–37.
Buonfino, A., and G. Mulgan. 2009. *Civility lost and found.* London: Young Foundation.
Cameron, D. 2001. *Working with spoken discourse.* London: Sage.
Chen, G.M. 2011. Tweet this: A uses and gratifications perspective on how active Twitter use gratifies a need to connect with others. *Computers in Human Behavior* 27 (2): 755–762. doi:10.1016/j.chb.2010.10.023.
Chun, E., and K. Walters. 2011. Orienting to Arab orientalisms: Language, race, and humour in a YouTube video. In *Digital discourse: Language in the new media*, ed. C. Thurlow and K. Mroczek, 251–273. Oxford: Oxford University Press.
Clark, H.H., and T.B. Carlson. 1982. Hearers and speech acts. *Language* 58 (2): 332–373.
Cohen, L. 2015. World attending in interaction: Multitasking, spatializing, narrativizing with mobile devices and Tinder. *Discourse, Context and Media* 9: 46–54.
Conover, M.D., J. Ratkiewicz, M. Francisco, B. Gonçalves, A. Flammini, and F. Menczer. 2011. Political polarization on Twitter. In *Proceedings of the 5th international AAAI conference on weblogs and social media*, 89–96.
Cook, G. 1989. *Discourse.* Oxford: Oxford University Press.
Cook, G. 1990. Transcribing infinity: Problems of context presentation. *Journal of Pragmatics* 14 (1): 1–24.
Couldry, N. 2008. Mediatization or mediation: Alternative understandings of the emergent space of digital storytelling. *New Media & Society* 10 (3): 373–391.
Coupland, N. 2003. Sociolinguistic authenticities. *Journal of Sociolinguistics* 7: 417–431.
Coupland, N. 2014. Social context, style and identity in sociolinguistics. In *Research methods in sociolinguistics*, ed. Janet Holmes and Kirk Hazen, 290–303. Malden, MA: Wiley-Blackwell.
Crystal, D. 2003. *A dictionary of linguistics and phonetics.* Cambridge: Cambridge University Press.
Crystal, D. 2006. *Language and the internet*, 2nd ed. Cambridge: Cambridge University Press.

Crystal, D. 2011. 'O brave new world, that has such corpora in it!': New trends and traditions on the internet. Plenary paper given to ICAME 32. Trends and Traditions in English Corpus Linguistics, Oslo, 1 June.

Darics, E. 2010. Politeness in computer-mediated discourse of a virtual team. *Journal of Politeness Research* 6 (1): 129–150.

Denscombe, M. 2004. *The good research guide: For small-scale social research projects*, 2nd ed. Maidenhead: Open University Press.

Deumert, A. 2014. *The sociolinguistics of mobile communication*. Edinburgh: Edinburgh University Press.

Doward, J. 2013. Twitter under fire after bank note campaigner is target of rape threats. *The Guardian*, July 27. www.theguardian.com/uk-news/2013/jul/27/twitter-trolls-threats-bank-notes-austen. Accessed 27 Sept 2016.

Drasovean, A., and C. Tagg. 2015. Evaluative language and its community-building role on TED.com: An appraisal and corpus analysis. *Language@Internet*.

Duranti, A., and C. Goodwin (eds.). 1992. *Rethinking context: Language as an interactive phenomenon*. Cambridge: Cambridge University Press.

Eckert, P. 2012. Three waves of variation study: The emergence of meaning in the study of sociolinguistic variation. *Annual Review of Anthropology* 41: 87–100.

Ellison, N.B., J. Vitak, C. Steinfield, R. Gray, and C. Lampe. 2011. Negotiating privacy concerns and social capital needs in a social media environment. In *Privacy online*, ed. S. Trepte and L. Reinecke, 19–32. Berlin and Heidelberg: Springer.

Evans, M., and C. Tagg. 2016. Spellings in context: Trans-historical perspectives on written variation and identity in Tudor correspondence and 21st century text messages. Paper presented at historicising the digital: Language practices in new and old media. University of Leicester, June 27–28.

Facebook. 2012. Making your settings easier to find: Dig into the details. https://www.facebook.com/about/details/. Accessed 25 Nov 2011.

Farah, I. 1998. The ethnography of communication. In *Encyclopedia of language and education: Research methods in language and education*, vol. 8, ed. N.H. Hornberger and P. Corson, 125–127. Dordrecht: Kluwer.

Finegan, E., and D. Biber. 2001. Register variation and social dialect variation. In *Style and Sociolinguistic Variation*, ed. P. Eckert and J. R. Rickford, 235–267. Cambridge: Cambridge University Press.

Frobenius, M. 2014. Audience design in monologues: How vloggers involve their viewers. *Journal of Pragmatics* 72: 59–72.

García, O., and Li Wei. 2014. *Translanguaging: Language, bilingualism and education*. London: Palgrave.

Garfinkel, H. 1967. *Studies in ethnomethodology*. Englewood Cliffs, NJ: Prentice-Hall.

Garrett, R.K. 2009a. Echo chambers online? Politically motivated selective exposure among internet news users. *Journal of Computer-Mediated Communication* 14: 265–285.
Garrett, R.K. 2009b. Politically motivated reinforcement seeking: Reframing the selective exposure debate. *Journal of Communication* 59: 676–699.
Gee, J.P. 2005. Semiotic social spaces and affinity spaces: From the age of mythology to today's schools. In *Beyond Communities of Practice: Language, power and social context*, ed. D. Barton and K. Tusting, 214–232. Cambridge: Cambridge University Press.
Gee, J.P., and E.R. Hayes. 2011. *Language and learning in the digital age*. New York: Routledge.
Georgakopoulou, A. 1997. Self-presentation and interactional alignments in e-mail discourse: The style and code-switches of Greek messages. *International Journal of Applied Linguistics* 7: 141–164.
Georgakopoulou, A. 2017. Whose context collapse? Ethical clashes in the study of language and social media in context. *Applied Linguistics Review*. doi:10.1515/applirev-2016-1034.
Georgakopoulou, A., and T. Spilioti, (eds.). 2015. *The Routledge handbook of language and digital communication*. Abingdon: Routledge.
Gershon, I. 2010a. Breaking up is hard to do: Media switching and media ideologies. *Journal of Linguistic Anthropology* 20: 389–405.
Gershon, I. 2010b. Media ideologies: An introduction. *Journal of Anthropology* 20 (2): 283–293.
Gershon, I. 2010c. *The breakup 2.0: Disconnecting over new media*. Ithaca, NY: Cornell University Press.
Giaxoglou, K. 2017. Reflections on internet research ethics from language-focused research on web-based mourning: Revisiting the private/public distinction as a language ideology of differentiation. *Applied Linguistics Review*. doi:10.1515/applirev-2016-1037.
Giles, H., and P.F. Powesland. 1975. *Speech Style and Social Evaluation*. London: Academic Press.
Gilroy, P. 2004. *After empire: Melancholia or convivial culture?* London: Routledge.
Goffman, E. 1975. Replies and responses. *Language and Society* 5: 257–313.
Goffman, E. 1981. *Forms of talk*. Philadelphia: University of Pennsylvania Press.
Goodwin, C., and A. Duranti. 1992. Rethinking context: An introduction. In *Rethinking context: Language as an interactive phenomenon*, ed. A. Duranti and C. Goodwin, 1–42. Cambridge: Cambridge University Press.
Gottfried, J., and Shearer, E. 2016. News use across social media platforms 2016. *Pew Research Center* May 26. Retrieved from: https://www.journalism.org/2016/05/26/news-use-across-social-media-platforms-2016/.
Graddol, D., and J. Swann. 1989. *Gender voices*. Oxford: Blackwell.

Granovetter, M.S. 1973. The strength of weak ties. *The American Journal of Sociology* 78 (6): 1360–1380.
Grevet, C., L. Terveen, and E. Gilbert. 2014. Managing political differences in social media. In *Proceedings of the 17th ACM conference on Computer supported cooperative work & social computing*, 1400–1408, ACM.
Guest, G. 2012. *Applied thematic analysis.* Thousand Oaks, CA: Sage.
Gumperz, J. 1967. On the linguistic markers of bilingual communication. *Journal of Social Issues* 23 (1): 48–57.
Gumperz, J. 1982. *Discourse strategies.* Cambridge: Cambridge University Press.
Gumperz, J., and D. Hymes (eds.). 1972. *Directions in sociolinguistics: The ethnography of communication.* Holt: Rinehart and Winston.
Hall, K. 1996. Cyberfeminism. In *Computer-mediated communication: Linguistic, social and cross-cultural perspectives*, ed. S. C. Herring, 147–170. Amsterdam, Philadelphia: John Benjamins.
Halliday, M.A.K., and R. Hasan. 1976. *Cohesion in English.* London: Longman.
Halliday, M.A.K., and R. Hasan. 1985. *Language, context and text: Aspects of language in a social-semiotic perspective.* Geelong, VIC: Deakin University Press.
Hampton, K.N., L.S. Sessions Goulet, L. Rainie, and K. Purcell. 2011. Social networking sites and our lives. *Pew Research Center's Internet & American Life Project.* www.pewinternet.org/files/old-media//Files/Reports/2011/PIP%20-%20Social%20networking%20sites%20and%20our%20lives.pdf.
Hardaker, C. 2010. Trolling in asynchronous computer-mediated communication: From user discussions to academic definitions. *Journal of Politeness Research* 6: 215–242.
Hendus, U. 2015. See Translation: Explicit and implicit language policies on Facebook. *Language Policy* 14: 397–417.
Herring, S.C., D.A. Johnson, and T. DiBenedetto. 1995. This discussion is going too far! Male resistance to female participation on the internet. In *Gender articulated: Language and the socially constructed self*, ed. K. Hall and M. Bucholtz, 67–96. New York: Routledge.
Herring, S.C. 1999. The rhetorical dynamics of gender harassment on-line. *The Information Society* 15: 151–167.
Herring, Susan C. 1994. Politeness in computer culture: Why women thank and men flame. In *Cultural performances: Proceedings of the third Berkeley women and language conference*, ed. Mary Bucholtz, Anita Liang, Laurel Sutton, and Caitlin Hines, 278–294. Berkeley, CA: Woman and Language Group.
Hewson, C., and D. Laurent. 2008. Research design and tools for internet research. In *The SAGE handbook of online research methods*, ed. N. Fielding, R.M. Lee, and G. Blank, 58–79. London: Sage. doi:http://dx.doi.org/10.4135/9780857020055.

Hirzalla, F., L. van Zoonen, and F. Mueller. 2013. How funny can Islam controversies be? Comedians defending their faiths on YouTube. *Television and New Media* 14 (1): 46–61.

Hofer, M., and V. Aubert. 2013. Perceived bridging and bonding social capital on Twitter: Differentiating between followers and followees. *Computers in Human Behavior* 29: 2134–2142.

Horst, H., B. Herr-Stephenson, and L. Robinson. 2010. Media ecologies. In *Hanging out, messing around and geeking out: Kids living and learning with new media*, ed. M. Ito, et al., 32–78. Cambridge, MA: MIT Press.

Hunston, S. 2002. *Corpora in applied linguistics*. Cambridge: Cambridge University Press.

Hymes, D. 1972. On communicative competence. In *Sociolinguistics: Selected readings*, ed. J.B. Pride and J. Holmes, 269–293. Harmondsworth: Penguin.

Hymes, D. 1974. *Foundations of sociolinguistics: An ethnographic approach*. Philadelphia: University of Pennsylvania Press.

Hymes, D. 1977. Toward ethnographies of communication. In *Language and literacy in social practice*, ed. J. Maybin, 11–22. Bristol: Multilingual Matters.

Hymes, D.H. 1972. Models of the interaction of language and social life. In *Directions in sociolinguistics: The ethnography of communication*, ed. J.J. Gumperz and D. Hymes, 35–71. New York: Holt, Rinehart and Winston.

Independent. 2016. Mark Zuckerberg admits Facebook must do more to police hate speech against refugees, February 27 2016. http://www.independent.co.uk/news/people/mark-zuckerberg-admits-facebook-must-do-more-to-police-hate-speech-against-refugees-a6899876.html.

Isaac, M. 2016. Facebook, in Cross Hairs After Election, Is Said to Question Its Influence. *The New York Times* November 14. Available at https://www.nytimes.com/2016/11/14/technology/facebook-is-said-to-question-its-influence-inelection.html?.

Ito, M., et al., 2010. Hanging out, messing around and geeking out: Kids living and learning with new media. Cambridge, MA: MIT Press.

Iyengar, S., and K.S. Hahn. 2009. Red media, blue media: Evidence of ideological selectivity in media use. *Journal of Communication* 59: 19–39.

Iyengar, S., K.S. Hahn, J.A. Krosnick, and J. Walker. 2008. Selective exposure to campaign communication: The role of anticipated agreement and issue public membership. *Journal of Politics* 70: 186–200.

Jeong Y., and E. Coyle. 2014. What are you worrying about on Facebook and Twitter? An empirical investigation of young social network site users' privacy perceptions and behaviors. *Journal of Interactive Advertising* 14 (2): 51–59.

John, N.A., and S. Dvir-Gvirsman. 2015. I don't like you any more: Facebook unfriending by Israelis during the Israel-Gaza conflict of 2014. *Journal of Communication* 65 (6): 953–974.

Johnson, I. 2013. Audience design and communication accommodation theory: Use of Twitter by Welsh-English biliterates. In *Social media and minority languages: Convergence and the creative industries*, ed. E.H.G. Jones and E. Uribe-Jongbloed, 99–118. Bristol: Multilingual Matters.

Jones, R. 2004. *Sites of engagement as sites of attention: Time, space and culture in electronic discourse*. Paper presented at AAAL, Portland, Oregan, 2004.

Jones, R. 2009. Dancing, skating and sex: Action and text in the digital age. *Journal of Applied Linguistics* 6 (3): 283–302.

Jones, R., and C. Hafner. 2012. *Understanding digital literacies: A practical introduction*. Abingdon: Routledge.

Jurgenson, N. 2012. The IRL fetish. *The new inquiry*. http://thenewinquiry.com/essays/the-irl-fetish/. Accessed 2 Sep 2013.

Keane, Webb. 2003. Semiotics and the social analysis of material things. *Language & Communication* 23 (2/3): 409–425.

Kosinski, M., D. Stillwell, and T. Graepel. 2013. Private traits and attributes are predictable from digital records of human behavior. *Proceedings of the National Academy of Sciences of the Unites States of America* 110: 5802–5805.

Kytölä, S. forthcoming. Race talk in discourse of football in digital media. In *Routledge handbook of language and superdiversity*, ed. A. Creese. London: Routledge.

Labov, W. 1966. *The social stratification of English in New York City*. Washington, DC: Center for Applied Linguistics.

Labov, W. 1972. *Sociolinguistic patterns*. Philadelphia: University of Pennsylvania Press.

Lang, C., and H. Barton. 2015. Just untag it: Exploring the management of undesirable Facebook photos. *Computers in Human Behavior* 43: 147–155.

Lange, P.G. 2014. Commenting on YouTube rants: Perceptions of inappropriateness or civic engagement? *Journal of Pragmatics* 73: 53–65.

Lee, C. 2007. Linguistic features of email and ICQ instant messaging in Hong Kong. In *The multilingual internet: Language, culture, and communication online*, ed. B. Danet and S.C. Herring, 184–208. Oxford: Oxford University Press.

Lee, C. 2007. Affordances and text-making practices in online instant messaging. *Written Communication* 24: 223–249.

Lee, E.-J. 2007. Deindividuation effects on group polarization in computer-mediated communication: The role of group identification, public self-awareness and perceived argument quality. *Journal of Communication* 57: 385–403.

Leppänen, S., S. Kytölä, H. Jousmäki, S. Peuronen, and E. Westinen. 2014. Entextualisation and resemiotization as resources for identification in social media. In *The language of social media: Identity and community on the internet*, ed. P. Seargeant and C. Tagg, 112–138. Basingstoke: Palgrave.

Leppänen, S., E. Westinen, and S. Kytölä (eds.). 2017. *Social media discourse, (dis)identifications and diversities.* Abingdon: Routledge.

Liu, Z., and Weber, I. 2014. Is Twitter a public sphere for online conflicts? A cross-ideological and cross-hierarchical look. In *Social informatics: 6th international conference*, ed. L.M. Aiello and D. McFarland, 336–347, SocInfo 2014, Barcelona, Spain, Nov 11–13, 2014. Proceedings. Cham: Springer International Publishing.

Locher, M.A., and R.J. Watts. 2005. Politeness theory and relational work. *Journal of Politeness Research* 1 (1): 9–33.

Locher, M.A. 2006. Polite behaviour within relational work: The discursive approach to politeness. *Multilingua* 25: 249–267.

Lofland, H. 1989. Social life in the public realm. A review. *Journal of Contemporary Ethnography* 17: 453–482.

Lofland, L.H. 1998. *The public realm: Exploring the city's quintessential social territory.* Hawthorne, NY: Aldine de Gruyter.

Lorenzo-Dus, N., P. Garcés-Conejos Blitvich, and P. Bou-Franch. 2011. On-line polylogues and impoliteness: The case of postings sent in response to the Obama Reggaeton YouTube video. *Journal of Pragmatics* 43 (10): 2578–2593.

Luzón, M.J. 2013. 'This is an erroneous argument': Conflict in academic blog discussions. *Discourse, Context and Media* 2: 111–119.

Lyons, A. 2014. *Self-presentation and self-positioning in text-messages: Embedded multimodality, deixis, and reference frame.* Unpublished PhD thesis, School of Languages, Linguistics & Film, Queen Mary University of London.

Lyons, A. and C. Tagg (in preparation). Mico-entrepreneurs and the language of business-related communication via mobile messaging apps.

Mackenzie, J. 2017. Identifying informational norms in Mumsnet Talk: A reflexive-linguistic approach to internet research ethics. *Applied Linguistics Review.* doi:10.1515/applirev-2016-1042.

MacKinnon, R. 2011. *Consent of the networked.* New York: Basic Books.

Madianou, M. 2012. News as a looking glass: Shame and the symbolic power of mediation. *International Journal of Cultural Studies* 15 (1): 3–16.

Madianou, M., and D. Miller. 2012. Polymedia: Towards a new theory of digital media in interpersonal communication. *International Journal of Cultural Studies* 16 (2): 169–187.

Malinowski, B. 1923. The problem of meaning in primitive languages. In *The meaning of meaning: A study of the infroence of language upon thought and of the science of symbolism*, ed. C.K. Ogden and I.A. Richards, 296–336. London: Kegan Paul, Trench, Trubner.

Marwick, A., and D. boyd. 2011. I tweet honestly, I tweet passionately: Twitter users, context collapse, and the imagined audience. *New Media & Society* 13 (1): 114–133.

Marwick, A., and D. boyd. 2014. Networked privacy: How teenagers negotiate context in social media. *New Media & Society* 16 (7): 1051–1067.

McLaughlin, C., and J. Vitak. 2012. Norm evolution and violation on Facebook. *New Media & Society* 14: 299–315.

Meyrowitz, J. 1985. *No sense of place: The impact of electronic media on social behavior*. New York: Oxford University Press.

Miller, D. 2016. *Social media in an English village*. London: UCL Press.

Miller, D., and J. Sinanan. 2014. *Webcam*. Cambridge: Polity Press.

Monaghan, F. 2014. Seeing red: Social media and football fan activism. In *The language of social media: Identity and community on the Internet*, ed. P. Seargeant and C. Tagg, 228–254. Basingstoke: Palgrave Macmillan.

Moor, P.J., A. Heuvelman, and R. Verleur. 2010. Flaming on YouTube. *Computers in Human Behavior* 26: 1536–1545.

Moore, S. 2004. The doubling of place: Electronic media, time-space arrangements and social relationships. In *MediaSpace: Place, scale and culture in a media age*, ed. N. Couldry and A. McCarthy, 21–36. London: Routledge.

Mullen, T. 2016. Hundreds of Pokemon Go incidents logged by police. *BBC News Online*, August 29. www.bbc.co.uk/news/uk-england-37183161.

Newon, L. 2011. Multimodal creativity and identities of expertise in the digital ecology of a World of Warcraft guild. In *Digital discourse: Language in the new media*, ed. C. Thurlow and K. Mroczek, 131–153. Oxford: Oxford University Press.

Nissenbaum, H. 2010. *Privacy in context: Technology, policy, and the integrity of social life*. Palo Alto: Stanford Law Books.

Noble, G. 2009. Everyday cosmopolitanism and the labour of intercultural community. In *Everyday multiculturalism*, ed. A. Wise and S. Velayutham, 46–65. Basingstoke: Palgrave Macmillan.

Ochs, E. 1979. Introduction: What child language can contribute to pragmatics. In *Developmental pragmatics*, ed. E. Ochs and B. Schiefflin, 1–17. New York: Academic Press.

Page, R. 2014a. Hoaxes, hacking and humour: Analysing impersonated identity on social network sites. In *The language of social media: Identity and community on the internet*, ed. P. Seargeant and C. Tagg, 46–64. London: Palgrave.

Page, R. 2014b. Saying sorry: Corporate apologies posted on Twitter. *Journal of Pragmatics* 62: 30–45.

Pihlaja, S. 2011. Cops, popes, and garbage collectors: Metaphor and antagonism in an atheist/Christian YouTube video thread. *Language@Internet* 8. http://www.languageatinternet.org/articles/2011/Pihlaja. Accessed Feb 19 2014.

Pihlaja, S. 2016. Expressing pleasure and avoiding engagement in online adult video comment sections. *Journal of Language and Sexuality* 5 (1): 94–112.

Pihlaja, S. forthcoming. More than fifty shades of grey: Copyright on social network sites. *Applied Linguistics Review*.

Pihlaja, S. 2014. *Antagonism on YouTube: Metaphor in online discourse*. London: Bloomsbury.
Piwek, L., and A. Joinson. 2015. What do they snapchat about? Patterns of use in time-limited instant messaging service. *Computers in Human Behavior* 54: 358–367.
Podesva, R.J. 2007. Phonation type as a stylistic variable: The use of falsetto in constructing a persona. *Journal of Sociolinguistics* 11 (4): 478–504.
Rainnie, L., and A. Smith. 2012. Social networking sites and politics. *Pew Internet Report*. http://pewinternet.org/Reports/2012/Social-networking-and-politics.aspx.
Reicher, S.D., R. Spears, and T. Postmes. 1995. A social identity model of deindividuation phenomena. *European Review of Social Psychology* 6 (1): 161–198.
Renninger, B.J. 2015. "Where I can be myself.. where I can speak my mind": Networked counterpublics in a polymedia environment. *New Media & Society* 17 (9): 1513–1529.
Sacks, H., E. Schegloff, and G. Jefferson. 1974. A simplest systematics for the organisation of turn-taking for conversation. *Language* 50: 696–735.
Schieffelin, B., and R. Doucet. 1998. The "real" Haitian Creole: Ideology, metalinguistics, and orthographic choice. *In Language Ideologies: Practice and theory*, ed. B. Schieffelin, K.A. Woolard, and P.V. Kroskrity, 285–316. New York: Oxford University Press.
Seargeant, P., C. Tagg and W. Ngampramuan. 2012. Language choice and addressivity strategies in Thai-English social network interactions. *Journal of Sociolinguistics* 16 (4): 510–531.
Silverstone, R. 2002. Complicity and collusion in the mediation of everyday life. *New Literary History* 33 (5): 745–764.
Sleeper, M., R. Balebako, S. Das, A.L. McConahy, J. Wiese and L.F. Cranor. 2013. The post that wasn't: Exploring self-censorship on Facebook. In *Proceedings of the 2013 conference on computer supported cooperative work* 13: 793–802.
Solon, O. 2016. Facebook's failure: Did fake news and polarized politics get Trump elected? *The Guardian* November 10. Retrieved from: https://www.theguardian.com/technology/2016/nov/10/facebook-fake-news-election-conspiracy-theories?.
Spilioti, T., and C. Tagg. 2016. The ethics of online research methods in applied linguistics: Challenges, opportunities, and directions in ethical decision-making. *Applied Linguistics Review* doi:10.1515/applirev-2016–1033.
Spitulnik, D. 2010. Millennial encounters with mainstream television news: Excess, void, and points of engagement. *Journal of Linguistic Anthropology* 20 (2): 372–388.
Sunstein, C. 2002. *Republic.com*. Princeton, NJ: Princeton University Press.

Sutton, L. A. 1999. All media are created equal. Do-it-yourself identity in alternative publishing. In *Reinventing Identities: The Gendered Self in Discourse*, ed. M. Bucholtz, A.C. Liang, and L.A. Sutton, 163–180. New York, Oxford: Oxford University Press.

Sveningson, M. 2014. I don't like it and I think it's useless, people discussing politics on Facebook: Young Swedes' understandings of social media use for political discussion. *Cyberpsychology: Journal of Psychosocial Research on Cyberspace* 8 (3).

Tagg, C. 2013. Negotiating social roles in semi-public online contexts. Talk given at *Conceptualizing multilingualism under superdiversity: Membership claims, social categories and emblems of authenticity*, June 11–12. University of Birmingham.

Tagg, C. 2016. Heteroglossia in text-messaging: Performing identity and negotiating relationships in a digital space. *Journal of Sociolinguistics* 20 (1): 59–85.

Tagg, C., and P. Seargeant. 2014. Audience design and language choice in the construction and maintenance of translocal communities on social network sites. In *The language of social media: Identity and community on the internet*, ed. P. Seargeant and C. Tagg, 161–185. Basingstoke: Palgrave Macmillan.

Tagg, C. and P. Seargeant. 2016. Facebook and the discursive construction of the social network. In *The Routledge handbook of language and digital communication*, ed. A. Georgakopoulou and T. Spilioti, 339–353. Abingdon: Routledge.

Tagg, C., and P. Seargeant. 2017. Negotiating social roles in semi-public online contexts. In *Social media discourse, (dis)identifications and diversities*, ed. S. Leppänen, S. Kytölä, and E. Westinen, 211–234. Abingdon: Routledge.

Takahashi, T. 2010. MySpace or Mixi? Japanese engagement with SNS (social networking sites) in the global age. *New Media & Society* 12 (3): 453–475.

Takahashi, T. 2014. Youth, social media and connectivity in Japan. In *The Language of Social Media: Identity and community on the internet*, ed. P. Seargeant, and C. Tagg, 186–207. Basingstoke: Palgrave.

The Guardian. 2015. Taylor Swift and Nicki Minaj trade Twitter barbs over VMA nominations, July 21. https://www.theguardian.com/music/2015/jul/21/taylor-swift-nicki-minaj-twitter-feud-vma-awards. Accessed Nov 25 2016.

Thorne, S.L. 2008. Transcultural communication in open internet environments and massively multiplayer online games. In *Mediating discourse online*, ed. S. Magnan, 305–327. Amsterdam: John Benjamins.

Thurlow, C., and A. Jaworski. 2011. Banal globalisation? Embodied actions and mediated practices in tourists' online photo sharing. In *Digital discourse: Language in the new media*, ed. C. Thurlow, K. Mroczek, 220–250. Oxford: Oxford University Press.

Tiidenberg, K. 2015. Boundaries and conflict in a NSFW community on tumblr: The meanings and uses of selfies. *New Media & Society*, 1–16. doi:10.1177/1461444814567984.

Trudgill, P. 1974. *The social differentiation of English in Norwich.* Cambridge: Cambridge University Press.

Turkle, S. 1995. *Life on the screen: Identity in the age of the internet.* New York: Touchstone.

Turkle, S. 2012. *Alone together: Why we expect more from technology and less from each other.* New York, NY: Basic Books.

Valentine, G. 2008. Living with difference: Reflections on geographies of encounter. *Progress in Human Geography* 32: 323–337.

Valentine, G. 2014. Encounters in an age of diversity: Reflections on spatial normativities in public life and the future of social relations. Paper presented at *Superdiversity: Theory, method and practice*, June 23rd–25th 2014, University of Birmingham.

van Zoonen, L., F. Viz, and S. Mihelji. 2011. YouTube interactions between agonism, antagonism and dialogue: Video responses to the anti-Islam film Fitna. *New Media & Society* 13 (8): 1283–1300.

Varis, P., and X. Wang. 2011. Superdiversity on the internet: A case from China. *Diversities* 13 (2): 71–83.

Verschueren, J. 2010. Interactional sociolinguistics. In *Society and language use*, ed. J. Jaspers, J.-O. Östman, and J. Verschueren, 169–175. Amsterdam: John Benjamins.

Vertovec, S. 2007. Super-diversity and its implications. *Ethnic and Racial Studies* 30 (6): 961–978.

Vinagre, M. 2008. Politeness strategies in collaborative e-mail exchanges. *Computers & Education* 50 (3): 1022–1036.

Walton, S., and A. Jaffe. 2011. "Stuff white people like": Stance, class, race and internet commentary. In *Digital discourse: Language in the new media*, ed. C. Thurlow and K. Mroczek, 199–219. Oxford: Oxford University Press.

Watts, Richard J. 1989. Relevance and relational work: Linguistic politeness as politic behavior. *Multilingua* 8 (2–3): 131–166.

Wesch, M. 2009. YouTube and you: Experiences of self-awareness in the context collapse of the recording webcam. *Explorations in Media Ecology*, 19–34.

Wessendorf, S. 2014a. Being open, but sometimes closed. Conviviality in a super-diverse London neighbourhood. *European Journal of Cultural Studies* 17 (4): 392–405.

Wessendorf, S. 2014b. *Commonplace diversity: Social relations in a super-diverse context.* Springer.

Wessendorf, S. 2015. All the people speak bad English: Coping with language differences in a super-diverse context. *IRiS Working Paper Series* no. 9/2015, 1–20.

Williams, R. 1977. *Marxism and literature*. Oxford: Oxford University Press.

Wise, A. 2007. Multiculturalism from below: Transversal crossings and working class cosmopolitans. Paper presented at the COMPAS annual conference, July 5–6, Oxford University, Oxford.

Young, M.W. 1987. Malinowski and the function of culture. In *Creating culture: Profiles in the study of culture*, ed. D.J. Austin-Broos, 124–140. London: Allen and Unwin.

Youssef, V. 1993. Children's linguistic choices: audience design and societal norms. *Language in Society* 22 (2): 257–274.

Zappavigna, M. 2014. Coffee Tweets: Bonding around the bean on Twitter. In *The language of social media: Identity and community on the internet*, ed. P. Seargeant, and C. Tagg, 139–160. London: Palgrave.

Zillman, C. 2016. Hillary Clinton's "Delete Your Account" Tweet sparks an epic Twitter war with Trump. *Fortune*, June 10. http://fortune.com/2016/06/10/donald-trump-twitter-hillary-clinton/. Accessed Nov 25 2016.

Zimmer, M. 2010. But the data is already public: On the ethics of research in Facebook. *Ethics and Information Technology* 12: 313–325.

Index

A
Addressivity, 22
Affiliation, 46, 48, 72, 73, 104
Affordances, 3, 5–7, 9, 10, 13, 17, 20, 21, 24, 38, 40, 41, 45, 46, 48–50, 52–54, 71, 75, 76, 81, 94, 98, 103, 107, 108, 110, 113–115, 117–121
Agency, 1, 13, 16, 32, 41, 117, 121
Aggression, 2, 16, 44, 46, 47, 50, 116, 118
Algorithm, 5, 110, 119–121
Androutsopoulos, Jannis, 4, 32, 33, 35, 36, 39, 53, 54, 56, 108
Audience, 2, 3, 5, 11, 13, 17, 19–24, 28, 32–37, 40, 41, 45, 49, 53, 55–57, 67, 69, 70, 72, 75, 78, 81, 87, 93, 102, 103, 105, 106, 115, 121
Audience design, 22–24, 34, 37
Awareness, 3, 4, 7, 13, 14, 19, 24, 33, 37, 40, 41, 67, 69, 70, 76, 78, 79, 87, 88, 93, 99, 101, 103–105, 109, 110, 117, 120, 121

B
Bell, Allan, 5, 20, 22–24, 35, 37
Blocking, 94, 96, 100, 108, 109
Blommaert, Jan, 5, 35, 38, 39, 73
boyd, danah, 5, 9, 20–23, 32, 33, 76, 78, 106

C
Channel, 6, 9, 25, 28, 32, 38, 83
Civility, 90, 91
Context, 1, 2, 5, 9–11, 17, 19–37, 39, 41, 45, 46, 49, 51, 68–71, 75, 76, 79, 80, 83, 85, 87, 89, 91, 96, 98, 103, 107, 110, 119, 121
Context collapse, 5, 19–22, 24–26, 33, 35, 54
Context design, 1, 2, 5, 14, 19, 20, 29, 35, 36, 38, 41, 43, 44, 51, 52, 69, 70, 76, 79, 80, 87, 92, 100, 106, 107, 109, 110, 115, 116, 118, 121
Contextualistion cues, 30, 81, 118
Conviviality, 44, 55, 91, 93, 102, 108–110, 115, 116, 118, 119

138 INDEX

Co-text, 26, 27
Creating Facebook project, 45, 51
Critical digital literacy, 10
Crossposting. *See* Transposting

D
Deindividuation, 46
Difference, 4, 7, 24, 50, 53, 54, 67, 82, 89–91, 93, 113, 118
Disidentification, 77, 85

E
Echo chamber, 48
Ego-centred, 4, 54, 55, 89, 118
Entextualisation, 33, 39, 40, 107

F
Facebook, 1–15, 17, 19, 21–24, 27, 33–42, 44, 45, 49, 51–59, 61, 63–90, 92–102, 104–111, 113, 115–121
Facebook group, 79, 97, 101, 107
Fake news, 3, 99
Fear of entextualisation, 76
Filter bubble, 48, 119
Flaming, 46, 47, 55, 116
Friends, 12, 14, 24, 31, 34, 37–40, 43, 50, 54–58, 61, 65, 67, 69, 72–77, 81–83, 88, 93–95, 103–106, 108–110, 118

G
Georgakopoulou, Alexandra, 5, 12, 30
Ghetto-ization, 4, 118
Goffman, Erving, 23, 30

H
Homophobia, 71, 95
Hymes, Dell, 28, 29, 34

I
Identification, 38, 78, 79, 87
Identity, 14, 38, 46, 55, 72, 80, 85, 87, 92, 104, 114
Ideologies, 1, 2, 5, 6, 8, 11, 35, 51, 106, 111
Impoliteness, 44
Instagram, 9, 70, 114, 117
Interactional sociolinguistics, 30
Intradiversity, 2, 4, 40, 53, 58, 67, 68, 70, 74, 110, 117

L
Liking, 36, 84

M
Media ecology, 2, 6, 9, 10, 17
Media ideologies, 6, 7, 15, 20, 38, 90, 94, 108, 110, 114
Mediascape, 117
Mediation, 10, 99
Meme, 39, 100, 114
Miscommunication, 2, 66, 81
Mode, 24, 25

N
Network, 3, 4, 11, 12, 14, 17, 24, 35, 40, 54, 56
Networked individualism, 54
Networked privacy, 21, 34, 78
Newsfeed, 3, 4, 39, 54, 77, 93, 109, 111, 121
Norms of communication, 38, 110

O
Offence, 1–4, 13, 14, 16, 17, 44, 50, 51, 53, 68, 71, 72, 77, 96, 101, 116
Online communication, 1, 5, 11, 20, 26, 31, 45, 90, 118, 121

Online–offline boundaries, 31
Overhearers, 23, 33, 55

P

Personalisation algorithm. *See* Algorithm
Pihlaja, Stephen, 46, 47
Pilot study, 13
Platform, 3, 6, 9, 10, 25, 47, 53, 115, 120
Politeness, 44
Politics, 48, 70, 72, 73, 75, 76, 87, 97, 106
Polycentricity, 35, 73
Polymedia, 9
Positive persona, 79, 86, 93
Privacy, 8, 14, 22, 34, 40, 50, 77–79, 87, 88, 92, 97, 104, 107, 108, 116, 120
Privacy settings, 14, 40, 50, 92, 107

Q

Questionnaire. *See* Survey

R

Racism, 96, 99
Recontextualisation, 82, 102
Reflexivity, 36, 41, 108
Relational work, 17, 43, 44
Religion, 73, 99

S

Self-presentation, 19, 20, 55, 79, 119
Semi-public, 19, 20, 24, 33, 50, 78, 83, 104
Sharing, 9, 33, 40, 56, 114

Skype, 115
Snapchat, 113, 115
Social media, 1–3, 5, 7, 10, 20, 21, 24, 32, 45, 89, 109, 114, 117
Social network site (SNS), 9, 51, 108
Social norms, 22, 45, 49
Sociolinguistics, 10, 19, 26, 29
Stance, 16, 43–45, 51, 89, 113
Status updating, 25, 33, 38
Style, 22, 23, 28, 35, 55, 100, 106
Stylisation, 37, 41
Superdiversity, 56
Survey, 1, 3, 13, 15, 47, 66, 69, 78, 106, 118

T

Technologies, 3, 7, 8, 11, 43
Technologisation of practice, 3, 8
Text, 8–10
Text Trajectories, 101
Thematic-discourse analytic approach, 15
Transposting. *See* Crossposting
Triviality, 85, 114
Twitter, 2, 7, 50, 54, 113, 116, 117

U

Unfriending, 94–97, 109

W

WhatsApp, 8, 24, 57, 115

Y

YouTube, 2, 4, 47–50, 54, 113, 116, 117